When Blessings Come..

Life becomes beautiful

RANJIT ARORA

Invincible Publishers

First published in India in 2018

ISBN: 978-93-87328-92-1

The author has tried to recreate events, locales and situations from his memories. In order to maintain anonymity, names of individuals etc have been changed. Some identifying characteristics/details, physical properties and names of places have been changed so as not to resemble any specific person/place.

Invincible Publishers

G-120, Sushant Lok III, Sector 57, Gurgaon-122002

Registered Address: Opposite Kasturba Ashram, Radaur, Haryana - 135133

Printed at Thomson Press (India) LTD

The book is primarily dedicated to my father, my hero, who taught me to invoke blessings from the Almighty in a very subtle manner. He taught me to live a life of courage and not to kowtow to anyone under pressure, but to go by my instincts. This is the year of his centenary celebrations.

The book is dedicated to my grand-daughters, Meher and Reet - my lucky mascots.

The book is as well dedicated to my wife who showed stoic patience in sitting by me while I wrote the book, and my sons and daughters-in-law who read the manuscript to ensure utmost accuracy.

And to my friend, Vijesh Gupta, who always stood by me as we complete fifty years of friendship.

ACKNOWLEDGEMENT

First of all, I express my gratitude to the Almighty for blessing me with the ability to write this book which I have titled 'When Blessings Come' on account of His blessings.

I am grateful to my editor, Aditi Saxena, for painstakingly and diligently editing the manuscript. The book would not have been complete without the interesting illustrations created by my colleague Mr. Deepak Verma who evolved himself as a designer in the process of helping me. The credit for designing the cover page also goes to him and Mr. Naved Akhtar for giving final touches to the design of the book.

I am also grateful to my publisher, Invincible Publishers, and Mr. Ajay Setia and his entire team who came forward to publish the book without even the slightest of inhibitions, even though I myself doubted whether I would be in a position to express my thoughts as conceived and conceptualized. The decision to publish the book was instantaneous after reading the first story.

Thanks to Mr. Pradeep Vohra and Nidhi Gupta who studied the entire manuscript to ensure that no omissions escaped our attention, and corrected them before the book went to the press.

PREFACE

I have often heard people say GOD BLESS YOU and seen messages like STAY BLESSED and wondered how God blesses or how we stay blessed. I couldn't comprehend the significance of these words, but I did have a feeling that it must not be for nothing that people say these words; it must have a deeper meaning. My quest to understand continued, and now I have reached that stage in my life when it has become amply clear that when you pray to God with a true heart and faith, He provides whatever you ask for. I would like to share that these phrases do have a deep significance. When I look back, I understand how and under what circumstances blessings come.

One incident that my father often narrated to me reinforces my belief that when God blesses you, He does it the way that serves you well, though it may be very difficult to connect the events at that time.

My father grew up in Amritsar and his entire education was imparted to him at home. He could

read, write and speak two languages – Urdu and Punjabi, and a smattering of Hindi. He was very good in mathematics.

He migrated from Amritsar to Delhi a few days after I was born. When he landed in Delhi at the age of 33, he had to find an employment. He contacted his relatives. His maternal uncle was an officer in the Indian Railways. As my father didn't have any school certificates, let alone a degree, his uncle could only get him a humble position job in the mechanical wing of the Railways.

We were a family of eight, our parents and six siblings, living in a railway quarter. The salary that he got at the end of each month was not adequate to meet the family expenses, and the shortfall had to be met by borrowing from the moneylender or the *bania* at an exorbitant rate of interest of 5% per month.

On each salary day, it was his practice to go to the *bania*'s shop and pay the interest on the outstanding along with some part of the amount due, and buy the provisions for that month. One of those months, he was left with no money after paying the instalment and the monthly interest. On his way to the bania's shop which was in a market, 500 metres from the residence, he wondered how he would settle the amount due and ask the *bania* to give the provisions as well. Lost in his thoughts, he looked towards the sky and prayed to God for his saving grace so that the *bania* would give him the provisions for feeding his family.

All of a sudden, he felt as if he had stepped on something. It was a small cylindrical packet wrapped in paper. He picked it up and opened the bundle to find two hundred-rupee notes. That was quite a sum at the time when the total bill for the monthly provisions used to be about Rs. 40. He looked around to see if somebody had dropped the money and was searching for it. There was nobody around. There was enough for him in the bundle; he could pay the interest of Rs. 5 and the full dues of Rs. 45 payable to the *bania*. Now, he walked confidently fully enthused and elated, to the *bania*'s shop and told him that he would like to pay off the entire dues with interest.

The *bania* was happy to hear that the entire outstanding amount was being realized along with interest. In return for full settlement of the long carried over debt, he offered my father to take provisions from his shop, even if he did not have any amount to pay thereafter.

My father stepped out of the *bania*'s shop feeling blessed, the divine had come to bless him and get him out of ignominy. He felt very confident that there was no challenge to provide for his family now onwards. He called it *Guru ki Meher* (Gift from the Master) and he often narrated this story to his offspring, inspiring them to have faith in the Almighty in all situations in life.

I had heard such narrations about blessings from my father and could only relate to them much later in life. It is a fact of life that when blessings come, life becomes beautiful. I have made a humble attempt to compile such incidents which changed the course of my life in the form of short stories, including also the stories of other people who shared such incidents from their lives with me.

We often worry about the problems that we encounter in our day-to-day lives, but if we surrender to the Almighty and pray to Him with full faith, he will provide for all our needs and desires.

Like me, I am sure the readers would have experienced similar situations, and as they read the stories, I hope they connect with such instances of blessings being showered on them.

CONTENTS

1. VALOUR 1
2. ART OF SHARING 7
3. EARLY SIGNS OF BLESSINGS 11
4. GOOD TEACHERS Vs. GREEDY TEACHERS 17
5. THE THREE MUSKETEERS 22
6. A CARING INVIGILATOR 28
7. FRENCH CARE 35
8. AN UNFORGETTABLE JOURNEY WITH A GIRL 41
9. ETIQUETTES 46
10. NO PROBLEM 53
11. SISU 60
12. STRANGERS –WHO BECAME FRIENDS 66
13. THE HONEST CAB DRIVER 72
14. DO UNTO OTHERS 79
15. THE TRAVESTY OF LAW 86

16. THANK YOU 91

17. FAUX PAS 98

18. NO GLITTER BUT SWEETER 103

19. MY FIRST BOOK 110

20. ANGUISH OF A LITTLE GIRL 115

21. THE CAR THAT CHANGED MY LIFE 121

22. THE PERKS OF BEING A SENIOR CITIZEN 127

23. FIGHTING DEPRESSION 133

24. POWER OF EMPATHY 139

25. A GREAT JOURNEY 146

1

VALOUR

When I was growing up, my father often narrated the following story to us and to our friends. He always encouraged us to live life with courage and often said, "You cannot live a day without God's will and nobody can cut short your destined life by even an hour, no matter if there are thousands of people against you."

The story goes as under:

"In the city of Amritsar, along a long but narrow street, there lived about a hundred families. We were quite unmindful of each other's religion, caste, or class, though the residents were predominantly Punjabis–Muslims or Hindus, with a few Sikh families.

We all lived together as a community with a lot of affection shared amongst us all.

However, the atmosphere changed all of sudden, which I noticed when I went to the river side for my routine morning walk. I met with some friends there, most of whom were Punjabi muslims, and was shocked to realize that their attitude towards me had changed overnight. They ignored my presence and acted dismissive. When I enquired about the reason behind such a behaviour, they expressed great anger and told me, "Your leader tore the Pakistani flag with a sword, therefore the entire Muslim community is very upset and has decided to boycott the entire Sikh community. We have been directed to keep away from all of you."

It was a sad day. 'How can my friends change their behaviour towards me over such a small incident, when I have nothing to do with it?' I kept thinking. I could not digest the fact that the relations which had developed over generations could be so fragile that the act of tearing a flag by one of our community leaders should put the families at loggerheads and snap the relationship all at once.

Days passed and we stopped talking to one another. The atmosphere got vitiated day by day with the rumours of partition, and the demand for a separate state by the Muslims. The leaders made provocative statements everyday and a sense of fear prevailed in the entire city. Our street was no better. The Muslims were in a majority there and felt all the more apprehensive regarding the impending waves of change. They knew that in the event of a partition, there was no chance that the city of Amritsar would be made part of the new homeland for Muslims. Amritsar was known to be the city of Sikhs and Punjabis.

But one gets used to life and accepts it as it comes, and people gradually got back to their regular business. Amritsar, at that time, was a major commercial city with a specialised market for each commodity, viz., flour (*Aata Mandi*), salt (*Namak Mandi*), rice (*Chawal Mandi*) and a myriad of similar bazaars. It was a flourishing centre for wholesale and retail business. I had my business in the chamber where we traded in wholesale commodities. The activity there used to be so hectic and engaging that once you were in the chamber, you tended to forget about life in the city outside.

One evening when I had almost finished with my day's trading activity, I enquired from my colleagues of what was going on in the city. They told me that the situation was very tense and the fact that most families were leaving the street where their community members were in a minority. That day being a Friday, a special namaz was announced for all the muslims to compulsorily attend.

It dawned on me that my wife was at home and our street had a majority of Muslims too. I immediately rushed back home to ensure that my family was safe. As soon as I entered the street, I saw a large congregation of Muslims outside the mosque, raising slogans against Indian leaders and chanting, '*Pakistan zindabaad*!' Hesitantly, I entered the street and stealthily made my way to the end of the street, at the corner of which stood my house. My wife was naturally very worried, however, my children were oblivious to the tense situation around and were playing. My daughter was a year and a half, while my son was only six months old.

I couldn't decide what to do under these circumstances. My wife suggested that we remain inside the house, switch off the lights so as to give the impression that we were not home. I was not in agreement with her view, since I was sure that some people must have noticed me entering the street. I also feared that if the gathering turned into a mob, they might even set the house on fire, since such incidents were quite common then. I could not tolerate the idea of the entire family being wiped off under such circumstances.

I prayed to God to protect us, then decided to leave the street at once. I took out my sword which I believed could certainly thwart people from attacking me. I had maintained it quite well. Everybody in the vicinity was aware that I was quite dexterous and skilful in handling swords and used to display my skill in the duels held in the *mohalla*.

I picked my son up in one arm, carried my naked sword in the other, and asked my wife to follow me out. I walked past the crowd without looking directly at anybody, but my sword did make a good show, threatening to deal with anybody who dared to come near us. My wife followed me in rapt silence. In a few minutes, we were out of the street and heaved a sigh of relief. A comment or slogan by even one person could have lead to a communal fight, and the situation could have turned very ugly.

The next morning, when I returned to my house, I had become a hero. The people of my community had heard about how I faced the tough situation and walked out of the street like a brave-heart.

Courage saved me that day and strengthened my belief that if God is on your side, nobody can harm you, even if there are a thousand people against you. This faith in God has guided me through life, making me fearless and always act with courage."

This story by my father got so entrenched in my psyche that it has always inspired me to live a life of courage and not to be cowed down under any circumstances.

2

ART OF SHARING

The art of sharing needs to be taught to children from a very young age, specially in the present times when households have shrunk to nuclear families and the young generation does not want to have more than two children. In metropolises and big cities, the preference is rather for a single child.

When we were growing up, we had one of our father's sisters staying in Lucknow. A very caring, loving and affectionate relationship was shared between my parents and my aunt's family. During our summer vacations, we would usually visit Lucknow for 3-4 weeks. Besides us, relatives from other stations also flocked there to spend the summer vacation together.

We addressed our aunt's husband as Darji. He always showered so much love and affection on all the children that we looked forward to spending our summer vacations at his place each year. Everyone in the family addressed him as Darji–even his own son and grand children. While our bhua (that is how we addressed our father's sister) prepared delicacies for us and made all the kids in the house come and sit on the floor in the kitchen to have the delicious breakfast, lunch and dinner, Darji would plan activities for us to pass the afternoons and evenings. It was great fun to be around so many of your kin, share the delicacies together and compete who could eat faster/more.

After the breakfast everyday, we would all assemble together and Darji would plan some game for everyone to participate in. Bhua ji relentlessly prepared new dishes everyday, and the fun and games would resume after each of her meal breaks. Darji was an industrialist and surely had a large income, as we never found them talking of how the expenditure on all this was to be met, in stark contrast to the scenario back at our home.

The post-lunch period used to be the most interesting time when we would all assemble in the *baithak* (the living room) for Darji to reveal a new game for us to play that day. With this story, I wish to recount one such game that was often played by us, in an effort by Darji to involve everybody. Today, when I sit back and recollect the contours of the game, I understand the underlying message that Darji had wanted to convey to all of us.

Darji would get a basket full of mangoes to the *baithak* and tell us that we could eat them, but it depended on our luck how many mangoes we got. Then, as part of the game, he would ask each one of us to pick up a slip (*parchi*) on which there was a number written. Turn by turn, we would pick up a slip each and whatever number was written on our slip, the same number of mangoes were given to the respective kid.

The number went up to even 20-25. Whoever picked the slip with such a large number and got that many mangoes, felt extremely happy, being almost a winner. However, when somebody opened their slip to find the number zero on it, tears rushed forth from the eyes and the victim cursed his luck in disappointment. Darji would come to the rescue then and offer a mango from his kitty, while also exhorting others to share their bounty if they so wished. As soon as even one of us shared a mango, a chain reaction would commence and even the zero-slip holder ended up with an equally large number of mangoes.

Darji rewarded the largesse shown with a special gift, given to the ones who had come forward to share the very first and the largest number of mangoes.

Thereafter, we would all spend the rest of the afternoon relishing the mangoes earned by us in the game. It really was a unique game that Darji played often, while teaching us subtly to share our belongings with our kin. To this day, I feel great pleasure when I find an opportunity to share with those who are less privileged. Perhaps this is due to the lesson that I had been taught at a very early stage in my life.

Those were the wonderful days spent in the company of such wise people who cared so much. They had the sagacity to teach us, ever so subtly, the values which got seeped so deep that even today, when I encounter a beggar or a needy person, the instinct to give is spontaneous.

3

EARLY SIGNS OF BLESSINGS

This story goes back to my school days. I was studying in a government school in Central Delhi, which was about 3 kms from my house. A few of us would walk to the school together, chit-chatting and enjoying each other's company. It was a middle school up to 8th standard under the 5+3+3 education system. I had joined the school in 6th standard after passing the board exams in 5th class from a primary school. In 6th standard, we were introduced to English language for the first time. It was not easy to score marks in the language subjects those days, as the teachers rarely fell in the generous category when it came to giving marks. 'Stingy' would best describe the way they marked us. As such, I had scraped through my 6th standard and was promoted to the next grade with just about passing marks.

A tragedy occurred in our family which transformed my life.

Besides the other siblings, I had a younger brother named Babbal. He was about two years younger to me, but far healthier and with a very fair complexion and robust demeanour. His presence created a feeling of inadequacy in me, because every relative would compare me with him and remark, 'How come you are so dark while your younger brother as well as the other kids in the family are so fair?'

As destiny would have it, Babbal suffered a high fever for a very long time, which was later diagnosed as typhoid. Despite the best treatment that we could afford at the Railway Hospital, his condition started deteriorating. Babbal didn't survive and during the period of mourning, I became a very serious child. I felt morose and carried a feeling of gloom and melancholy at that point of time. I felt that our happiness had been shattered by this tragedy in the family as Babbal was my companion at all times while playing, eating, going to school as well as sleeping.

When I returned to my school, my Maths teacher, while expressing his condolences, advised me to devote my time to studies and seek the company of good books.

Soon, we had our half-yearly exams and I found myself quite ill-prepared. As was customary, the first paper was that of English language. We were expected to write a short essay, a simple leave application, and then answer a few questions from the prose book prescribed in the curriculum. The last question was to write a short story, choosing from one of the three stories that we were taught as per the prescribed syllabus. I had not learnt any story and was about to hand over the answer sheet when I recalled the title of one of the stories–'Do Unto Others What You Would Have Them Do Unto You'. I could vividly recall the story and started writing it. After I had written the story as per the requirements of the question paper, I handed back the answer sheet, not expecting to be awarded any more than 2 or 3 marks, provided that the teacher didn't read it while checking

Soon, the exams were over and were followed by the holidays which were mostly spent playing all day long, besides a trip to Amritsar–our home town. When we returned to school after the holidays, a fear dawned over us as soon as the class teacher, who taught us English Language, entered the classroom. We noticed that he was carrying a bundle of sheets which naturally had to be our answer scripts.

After the attendance was over, he started calling out names to hand over the answer sheets with the marks obtained encircled prominently at the front. When my name was called out, I stood up to collect the answer sheet. I noticed a broad smile on the teacher's face, which was very rare, and he patted my back while handing over the answer sheet to me.

I returned to my desk and opened the script to check the marks. I was surprised to note that I had been awarded 8 marks out of 10 for the story. I was taken by surprise and completely amused. I wondered how he could award such high marks, since he always told us that for stories, it was difficult to get more that 50 percent marks. I couldn't control my astonishment and approached the teacher with my complaint that he had perhaps not read the story properly that I had written so casually, and that there could be no reason for him to assign such high marks for it. He heard me out. What he said then has stayed with me even till this day. I had written that story in my own understanding of the language, which was not expected of a student who had just started learning the language in the previous class. He mentioned that most of my classmates were given 3 to 5 marks as they had learned the story by heart and had reproduced it in their answer sheets. My language, he said, had an originality in its presentation and he felt happy that a student had made the attempt to write in this manner, and at such an early stage too. He expressed great appreciation for my attempt and exhorted me to read as many books as possible, learn new words and answer the questions in my own language from then on.

This gave me immense happiness and boosted my confidence. Since then, English became my favourite subject and I never looked back, always scoring high marks with ease. The story, however, taught me a great lesson which helped shape my life subconsciously.

4

GOOD TEACHERS Vs. GREEDY TEACHERS

Once you move to college after school, you often forget the names and faces of teachers who impacted and shaped your life, but the memories of some of them remain with you forever.

I remember those days vividly when I was studying in VIII standard in a Govt. school in Delhi. In those days, the Board Examinations used to be held in VIII standard. A new teacher had joined our school that year, who was made our class teacher and taught us science as well. He took a keen interest in teaching, discussed individually the problems of all the students and took pains to resolve them even after the school hours. Even when the schools closed a few days before the Board Examinations for the preparatory holidays, he would spend 4-5 hours with me every day to ensure that I was well prepared in every subject. The result was that when the board results were declared, I was pleasantly surprised to find out that I had topped the entire region.

In IX standard, I joined Ramjas School in Delhi and found most students in my class to have scored good marks in their VIII boards. In fact, there were about 12-14 students who even had a better percentage than mine. Despite having topped in my region, I was not even among the top ten students in this class. I resolved, however, to be among the top three when the IX standard results would be declared. It was a big challenge as back home, I had to spend about three to four hours after school everyday in domestic activities to provide financial support to my family.

This was the beginning of a bad phase in education, as teachers started giving tuitions outside of school and took little interest in teaching in the classrooms. I wouldn't put all the teachers in the same category, especially our Maths and English teachers who were fully dedicated in the class, and were always ready to help the students even after class. The other teachers, viz. the science subject teachers, had become greedy. By the time I entered XI standard, the evil of earning money from tuitions had caught up with most of the teachers and they compelled everyone in the class to join their tuition classes.

I achieved the milestone that I had set for myself and secured third position in my class in IX as well as X standard. I had refused to join any tuition during these two years. In XI standard however, some teachers went as far as declaring it in the class that they were not going to teach much at school and would only come to class to fulfil the formality, while the real teaching, methodically and systematically, would happen at their tuition classes. Everyone in my class joined the tuition classes, while I remained the odd man out. There was a lot of pressure on me as the teachers put out feelers through my other classmates that it would be very difficult for me to pass the XI standard board examinations if I did not join their tuitions. But I stood my ground and refused to be cowed down.

The day of reckoning arrived when the science teachers got together in the science lab and sent me a message to appear before them. When I did, they told me that I must join their tuition classes if I wanted to pass the examinations that year, otherwise I should be prepared to sit in the same class the next year. They told me that even the very poor students from my class had joined their tuition classes, so I, who appeared to come from a much better family background, should not have any problem in paying the tuition fee. They openly conveyed to me that they would not cover the entire syllabus in class, so there was little chance of my passing the board examinations.

At this point, I told them that I would not join their tuition classes no matter what approach they adopted to pressurize me, viz. not covering the entire syllabus in the classroom. I also challenged them that no student (except the one very serious and naturally brilliant student who had no other interests besides studies) would score more marks than me in the XI class Board examinations.

They were quite astonished with my response and perhaps had never imagined that a student, a mere teenager, could be so obdurate, that too while facing three teachers on the other side. They immediately changed their stand, appreciated my confidence and assured me their full support. They also offered to have me join their tuition classes and not pay at all, which I could make out was a façade, lest I go and complain to the Principal of the school. They asked me to feel free to seek their help whenever I faced any difficulty.

I started working very hard, increased my time for studying and eventually did well in the board exams. I waited with bated breath for the results thereafter.

The day finally arrived when the results were declared and I had indeed fared very well. I had stood second in my class. The teachers were all praise, specially the trinity (Physics, Chemistry and Mechanical Drawing) who invited me to the lab again and presented me with a bouquet. They showered me with accolades for my grit and determination and expressed that they had been humbled by my achievements. Fearing perhaps that I would spill the beans about them, they almost sang paeans in my praise, expressing that they rarely found a student like me who was so full of confidence and could deliver what he professed.

Nothing succeeds like success–was my learning from this phase of my life.

5

THE THREE MUSKETEERS

This story relates to the period of early seventies, when we had just moved from class X to class XI. During those days, schools had the 5 plus 3 plus 3 system, where we had board examinations at the end of class V, then in class VIII, and then again after class XI. It was, therefore, very important to score good marks in the class XI boards since the admission to colleges, engineering institutes including the IITs, and medical courses was based on these scores.

On graduating to the next class, the initial period used to be a very relaxed time. After the hard work for the previous year's final examinations and the results, about a month's time was taken over by preparing for the new class, buying books, getting acquainted with the new teachers and the environment, etc. By this time, the summer holidays would close in and all the serious studies would get postponed to the post-holiday period.

When I moved to XI standard, we had some new faces in our class. Soon, we found out that they were the students who couldn't qualify the previous board examinations and had to appear for them again with our batch. The three boys who had been detained were all good looking and appeared to be talented, but would earn the ire of the teachers because they had brought down the pass percentage of their class to a poor 92.5% from the near 100% status that the school otherwise enjoyed, specially in the science stream.

The pass percentage in board examinations was the yardstick to measure the reputation of a school and its teachers, while these boys had brought bad name to them by failing. For this reason, the teachers felt personally slighted by these three students.

I got to know them better with time and found out that their interests lay outside of books. One of these students was Anil–a tall, dark and lanky boy with a hair style that matched that of Dev Anand. Anil was very fond of movies and mimicry. He could act out any scene from any of Dev Anand's movies, imitating his gait and voice perfectly. Dev Anand was a superstar in those years, so smart and handsome that girls swooned while watching his movies.

Anil's father was a cobbler and had a very meagre income to bring up his family. He could not afford to enrol Anil for the tuitions that were given by the school teachers after school. Since the teachers wanted more and more students to attend their tuition classes, they often left the course material incomplete while teaching at school.

I developed an intimate friendship with Anil over time. He entertained me with his mimicry during recess and on our walks back home after school. His house was only a little distance away from mine. I started doing my bit to arouse Anil's interest in studies and helped him with the problems that he faced in Mathematics–which was my favourite subject. I was one of the A grade students of our class then. On top of that, our maths teacher was one of the

Three Musketeers
Show

best. He was so clever that only by reading the faces of the students, he could tell how much was being understood by whom. In his quintessential style, he would put a hand over his mouth to prevent the students from reading his lips, then point out with the stick in his hand the one whom he suspected had not understood anything, and he was generally correct. More often than not, Anil fell in this suspect category.

The other was Sheel–a very fair, short, but handsome boy who dreamt of becoming a film star. He came from a very well-to-do family; his father was a banker. Sheel despised wearing the school uniform. He would bring the school uniform in his bag and always be on the lookout to quickly change into it whenever the PT teacher came around to check. At times when he got caught, he would be caned on the hand, which was very painful. Yet, he could not be deterred from it and repeated the same routine the next day. Since the checking happened only once a week, he would roam about freely in class the next day, displaying his outfit fearlessly. He was very fond of listening to music and his favourite song was '*Chandi ki deewar na tori*'.

Though he was fair, handsome and very soft-spoken, the Maths teacher did not like his face at all since his score in maths had been very less in the previous year's board exams. I had to cover for him whenever the teacher wrote out a problem on the blackboard and asked one of the students to come and solve it. I would go running, unless he specifically pointed out Sheel who got very nervous in such situations.

The third was Mukesh–a very tall, fair and handsome boy with a very imposing personality. He did not look like a school student at all. His interest lay in singing and he could sing on a stage without any hesitation. He was a complete performer, knowing how to convey thoughts with his body language. We always looked forward to our Saturday meetings where the students performed by telling jokes, stories, singing, etc. No function or celebration was ever complete without Mukesh's song. His voice was mellifluous, resembling that of Talat Mehmood–a very popular singer of those times.

Even though all three of them were very talented in their own way, the teachers did not see any future for them. The only thing that mattered to them was their performance in the board exams. Today, when I see live performances of singers on shows like SA RE GA MA and Indian Idol, I feel that Anil, Sheel and Mukesh were born before the time.

I did appreciate the creative hobbies of these three musketeers, but I realised that they had to enhance their application level towards studies. A change did come about as I helped them with the subjects they encountered difficulties in. When the results for our board exams were declared, all three passed with good percentages.

I salute these classmates, the memories of whom I still cherish after more than four decades of our last association.

6

A CARING INVIGILATOR

An exam invigilator, exam proctor or exam supervisor is someone who is appointed by the examination board and services to maintain the proper conduct during an examination, in accordance with the exam regulations. It is the duty of the exam invigilator to monitor the examination candidates and prevent them from cheating during the exam. They are required to ensure that all the exams are carried out according to the rules set out by the exam board which allows each candidate to sit for the examination under the same conditions as the other candidates throughout the country.

There is a crucial phase in everyone's life when one is at the threshold of embarking upon one's career. The two years, from X to XII, give substantial stress to the parents as well as the students who find themselves in a quandary to decide between the options available, and whether the choice of a particular stream would lead to achieving success in the career that he desires or has aimed for.

When I passed out of my school, the competition was not so severe as it is today. With a little more than seventy percent marks in boards, my name was amongst the top ten in the list of students eligible for admission to a premier engineering college in Delhi and even had the option to pick the stream of my choice. My parents had no clue about higher education or career choices, and my father left it to me to decide where to go. He only had one suggestion to give, that I must choose the course which requires the minimum investment and in which I truly had

an interest. I was not too keen on engineering, so the best available alternative seemed to be going for graduation from a good college. I decided to pursue an Honours in Physics, Chemistry or Maths, as these were the most trending courses in those times. Even though I was very good at Mathematics and had more than 95% marks in the subject, I chose Physics since the career options were much better after pursuing this course.

It is a very critical and complex issue to decide the career path for one's offspring. Generally, parents want their children to choose a career that corresponds with the dreams they had for themselves, but couldn't pursue for various reasons. It is also natural for children, on the other hand, to align their dreams with what they see growing up in their contemporary times. The problem occurs when a child is pushed into a career which he/she doesn't like at all.

I was lucky since my parents didn't have any plans for me. Their only wish was for me to get into a good government/semi-government job which paid me adequate remuneration to bring up my family. With this freedom, I chose to study at Delhi University. While considering colleges, my preference leaned towards the colleges in North Campus and finally zeroed down on Hindu College. It was co-educational, had great faculty in the science stream, and had a reputation of having fairly superior cultural and sporting activities. Though the reputation of St. Stephen's college was at par or even slightly better in some areas, it was not co-ed back in those days, and was (in)famous for the snoot it begot in its students. Under such circumstances and all these constraints, my decision to opt for Hindu was perfect.

Though I had joined an Honours Course in Physics, where the students were expected to be all serious types with no interest in other activities like sports, politics or debate, our class stood as an exception to the status quo. In a matter of only a few days, we gelled quite well with each other. We faced the initial period of ragging boldly and could not be cowed down in front of the seniors. We would often go around the college in a big group, joking and laughing together.

The teachers of the Physics Department got worried and we heard them expressing their doubts whether we would be able to come up to everyone's expectations and keep up the college's reputation. One of our classmates' sister was a lecturer in the Mathematics Department in the same college. She once told her brother, "Your Physics Department teachers seem to be quite worried since your batch lacks the usual seriousness of a science class." They often said that our batch seemed no better than a BA Pass class where the students took admission in a good college only to add the college's brand to their own names.

However, when the first year's results were declared, the teachers were astonished. Students of our class had filled up the maximum positions in the university's top ten, more than any other college in the entire Delhi University.

The second year of college is generally taken quite lightly, since you have your achievements before you and you feel quite reassured that you have coped well with the life in college. The freedom that one acquires after starting college can sometimes lead one to the wrong track and many students take to drugs. The hostel students are particularly vulnerable to the risk of falling prey to such vices.

This little anecdote relates to my Statistics exam during the second year. We had two subsidiary papers, one in Chemistry and the other in Maths, besides the four papers in the core subject of Physics during the second year. In Maths, we had Statistics as one of the elective papers.

From our experience of the first year exams, we had learnt that how much you score in the exam is directly proportional to how much you can write during the three hour period. When I started answering the questions, I gauged that I would have to write with great speed as the paper was very lengthy and the only way to get through the exam was to accelerate the writing speed. Within the first hour, I had filled up the entire first sheet (containing 16 pages) and requested for an additional sheet (which had 4 pages). Within a few minutes, I asked for another sheet.

The invigilator was a young lady and a pretty good looking one too, though I had no time to appreciate her beauty at that time. Every time I requested an extra sheet, she delivered it efficiently, not engaging in the formality of signing log sheet for the requisition first.

Deeply engrossed in writing, I did not even notice that the invigilator had parked herself very close to my desk. When the time was about to be over, I happened to look up and the invigilator immediately kept an extra sheet on my desk. I told her that I didn't need it, to which she replied, "When you look up, you always ask for a sheet, so I positioned myself here to help you save a moment." Most students had already finished writing by then and were handing over their answer sheets one after the other. I thanked her profusely for her support and left the examination hall, feeling very satisfied.

I scored a distinction in that paper, which eventually changed the course of my life. After I completed my graduation in Physics, my parents insisted that I take up a job instead of going for higher studies, but I wanted to pursue a post graduation and decided to switch to Mathematics. Fortunately, Delhi University had evening classes for M.Sc. in Mathematics which suited me and I enrolled for the same.

My heart goes out to such people who derive satisfaction from their work by going the extra mile. With a little extra effort, some people help others to achieve great things in life without asking or holding any expectations in return.

Thank you, my caring invigilator and all such people.

7

FRENCH CARE

On completing my post graduation, I felt the need to expand my horizon in a new direction. Learning a new language appeared to be a good idea then to engage in and learn about another culture, another country, while also adding a new skillset to my credentials for better job opportunities. I explored some options and finally settled on learning the French language. After checking the avenues, I found that the best place to learn French was Alliance Française de Delhi, which is run by the French Embassy. Alliance Française was then located in South Extension in Delhi, one of the most posh areas of the city. It was easy to commute to the place too, since there was a direct bus from Red Fort (close to where I stayed) to South Extension.

The first day in class was quite interesting. Of about twenty-five students who had joined the batch, there were only seven or eight males, while the rest were girls. Our teacher was from Paris, France–a lean, very fair man who carried an air of snoot around him. He started his class by saying, "In this class, I speak only one sentence in English and that is, *Nobody will speak in English in this class from now on.*" We were all in a quandary; how could we have switched over to a new language from day one? Overawed and overwhelmed by such a declaration, we sealed our lips for the rest of the lecture.

One of my friends was learning the French language from another institute, so I decided to visit him and have a first hand report on how to tackle the situation. He gave me a book which had a glossary of French words with their pronunciations and meanings in English. He guided me on how to learn the language quickly by practicing by myself at home.

The next day at class, as soon as a student spoke a word or made an enquiry in English, the teacher shouted at him, “Shut up!” and he was thereby asked to leave the class for the day. In a matter of a week, most boys had left as they felt humiliated, specially in the presence of so many beautiful girls.

My plan, on the other hand, had worked quite well. I was able to construct small sentences in French and made queries to the teacher as well. All the girls were impressed with my progress and felt at ease that there was at least somebody in class who could interact with the teacher. As soon as the class would end, the girls scrambled for me with more than one girl claiming that it was her day to sit with me and take my guidance on the subject. It really put me on cloud nine.

After finishing school, I had joined a co-educational college to enjoy the company of the fairer sex, but the situation here was completely reversed. As the only male in an entire class of girls, I had to act like a real gentleman. On top of that, all these girls hailed from very good families. One of them was the daughter of Delhi city’s Mayor, another was the daughter of the Singapore ambassador, while some others worked at five star hotels and embassies.

At this stage, with our French teacher being the only other male in the classroom besides me, a

ALLIANÇE FRANCE DE DELHI

natural intimacy grew between us. Sometime later, I learnt that his girlfriend, who shared the same last name as him, had joined Alliance too. They had been in a live-in relationship for a number of years, but had not decided to tie the nuptial knots.

Soon after, another student joined and I got some good company to share. Since our class lasted for only an hour, we would head out thereafter to visit all the happening places in the city, be it exhibitions or cultural events. Our friendship soon grew into a very close relationship as we got to know each other better.

Meanwhile, I landed a job in a bank and left Delhi for it. A year and a half later, I came back to Delhi to join a State Bank branch in Central Delhi. I decided to return to Alliance and continue my French language classes, leaning on my luck to be placed in a similar situation again; the only male in a class full of beautiful women. I got what I had hoped for. The batch was predominantly all girls, with only one or two males who rarely came to attend the lecture, but the environment was very different this time. This batch had got a lady teacher who happened to be the girlfriend of my previous teacher. She was not very strict about her students interacting in English, though we had learnt enough French by then to be able to speak a few sentences.

This teacher was very nice to me. When she learnt that I had been a favourite student of her friend who had taught us earlier, she was very pleased. I soon became her favourite student too and she would go by my advice whenever we planned an outing or a cultural event with the batch.

The end of our session was drawing to a close and it was time for us to say goodbye to each other. Since we had developed such an intimate bond with each other as well as with our teacher, we decided to gift her a good sending-off present. After having collected the contribution amount from everyone, I suggested to the girls who were active with organizing events to get a good gift from the market in South Extension. What they said next took me completely by surprise. They said, "As long as the gift is your selection, she will love it."

"Why do you say so?" I enquired.

"You probably haven't noticed, but we have seen how her face lights up when she sees you in the classroom. The day you are not in class, her disappointment becomes apparent as soon as she enters the classroom. It's not easy to miss how her eyes are always searching for you in class," they said.

Although it was a bit embarrassing to know what my classmates revealed, it did give me immense happiness to know that my teacher had such affectionate feelings towards me. Some people hold affection, or a subtle connection, for us that we may not notice or be aware of.

I hold deep gratitude to her, as well as to all such people who harboured such feelings of care and affection for me, without me realizing it.

8

AN UNFORGETTABLE JOURNEY WITH A GIRL

Some people come to your life for a very short span of time and thereafter you miss them; you remember them, you want to reach out to them, but there is no way to make contact. When I sit and look back at my life now, I still revel in some beautiful moments given to me by a few people who touched my life and perhaps brought a great change in my life.

I was once traveling to Bhatinda from Delhi and had booked a sleeper berth in the train. Since I was going away from the family, I was feeling pretty morose, and then it was a night journey which I rarely enjoyed. To my pleasant surprise, however, there was a group of college students who had come to Delhi during their autumn break and were traveling back to their hometown in the same train. It was a large group of about twenty five with one male and one lady teacher accompanying them as their group leaders.

As expected from such a situation, the students were recalling the previous few days that they had spent in Delhi and were sharing some hilarious experiences which they had had in the city. There was a lot of hullabaloo in the coach with everybody trying to choose a proper berth; some preferred the lower berths, while the others wanted to relax on the upper berths to have an uninterrupted sleep.

I set my bed on the lower berth and watched the activity with great interest. I had joined my job at State Bank just about two years back and had been deputed after my probation to the Reserve Bank of India for conducting a survey. The geographical region that was allotted to me for this survey was Bhatinda and its satellite towns.

Luckily, I had a cousin staying in Bhatinda with her family. Her husband was a civil servant there. Thus, the hassle of finding a proper place to stay and have proper food was taken care of. This was what had brought me to travel in that train that night, and with such interesting company in that coach, I looked forward to a good time.

The teachers settled all the students on their respective berths, after which the lady teacher, who had joined the college as a teacher right after her post graduation a few months before, had no berth for herself and came to sit on my berth. She introduced herself and made herself comfortable, promising that she would move to another place whenever I want to stretch out and sleep.

Who would have wanted to sleep when one had a beautiful lady to chat with, and in such a romantic setting too. I assured her that I found it difficult to sleep in trains anyway. Moreover, I had nothing important to do the next day and could catch up on my sleep then.

We chatted the whole night and neither of us felt any need for sleep. It was the month of October and the weather grew colder as the night progressed. Octobers used to have a much cooler weather in the seventies and the early morning air used to be particularly chilling. The month of November heralded the arrival of winters then, making one require woollen clothing in Northern India.

The railways in those days did not provide any bedding or blanket, as is the system now. The coaches were not air conditioned. The second class sleeper and the first class had berths in the night trains, while for the day trains, there was only sitting. Fortunately, I was carrying my own blanket. When it grew slightly cold, we shared the blanket and the chatting continued. Lost in each other's words, we didn't notice which stations the train stopped at or what the next station was.

Before we could realize, it was already morning. The ticket collector arrived and announced that the train was about to stop at Maur station next. By this time, the male teacher had woken up too. When he heard that the train was to stop at Maur station, he got a little angry as the train had already moved past the station where their group was to get down. He enquired the same from the lady teacher, reproaching her whether she didn't know that they were to get down at Mansa. She expressed her apology and told him that she had got so engrossed in chatting with me that she did not notice which station had passed.

Another problem cropped up now. By protocol, they were required to pay an additional fare for travelling beyond their destination, and purchase the return tickets on top of that to board another train back to their actual destination. The ticket collector came to their rescue, however, and made a note on their tickets that the party comprising of these college students couldn't get down at their station as it was very early in the morning and still very dark outside so they missed their stop, and permitted them to travel back to their destination free of cost.

I was feeling very bad at this point because I felt responsible for having engaged her in chatting with me. When the next station arrived, the group disembarked the train and the male teacher thanked me, with sarcasm, for having shared my berth with his colleague and keeping her engaged in an interesting chat.

Thereafter, we never had a chance to meet. We only shared a few letters after that wherein she recollected the memories of that train journey, expressing that those were some of the best moments of her life. She also mentioned how she wished to relive such an experience again in her life.

I still cherish the moments spent chatting with her, when I look back and recollect the fond memories of that night. Despite not seeing her ever again, the chance meeting with her instilled in me the courage to approach new people without a tint of hesitation and develop new and lasting relationships.

9

ETIQUETTES

Etiquette is a beautiful word from the English language, pronounced as */etiket/* and is difficult to spell correctly unless you have come across the word often enough or have taken pains to memorise the spelling. Etiquette means (as per the dictionary) conventional rules of personal behavior in polite society.

Though I studied B.Sc. Physics Honours in college, followed by an M.Sc. in Mathematics, I often spent long hours in the library reading English Literature. Of all the books that I have read, two books that I hold as the best written are 'War and Peace' by Leo Tolstoy and 'Crime and Punishment' by Peter Dostoevsky. While I studied War and Peace during my post graduation years, Crime and Punishment fell into my hands in Kasauli. The latter book was so absorbing that I found myself in almost a trance like state, reaching for the book every morning as soon as I woke up and then again in the evening, as soon as I returned to my room from work. The book was so captivating that I missed my breakfast at times and on one occasion even dinner.

I was very lucky to have learned my lesson in etiquettes early in my career.

When I joined State Bank in the year 1977, the first branch where I was to undergo training was Kasauli, a picturesque town in the Solan District of Himachal Pradesh. It could perhaps have been a very boring time, had I not had two good habits–1. Love for nature, and 2. A hobby for reading.

On receiving the appointment letter, the probationers were required to report at the HO. Completing all the joining formalities thereafter, we were to report to the General Manager Planning (GMP) who briefed us on the career prospects and ways to adapt to the change which comes to life when one starts working. The GMP was a tall, lean and sophisticated gentleman who received every probationer individually by extending a warm welcome on behalf of the organization. He addressed everyone by their first names, making them feel quite assured that they had joined a great organization. He also mentioned that we shouldn't hesitate to write to him should we encounter any problem during the training period, or if the training schedule was not being adhered to.

During the first branch training, we had to attend an orientation programme where the State Bank stalwarts motivated us to embark upon our career paths by narrating their own success stories and hurdles that we were most likely to encounter during the course of our training. The Principal at the Staff College was again a very gentle and caring person who with his humility and care introduced us to the great career that lay ahead, working with the biggest bank in the country.

It so happened that during the month of March, five months after I joined the Kasauli branch, there was a long holiday and the Bank arranged for a Management Development Program for the senior and top management functionaries at Kasauli. While the

CUSTOMER MEET

GMP was to preside over the program, the Principal of the Staff College was invited as the Chief Guest as well as the co–ordinator for the program.

The Kasauli branch arranged a welcome party within its premises for the entire management team and we gathered outside the branch to receive about forty senior officers of the Bank. As soon as the GMP arrived and caught sight of me, he called out to me by my first name and asked me, “How are you?” This was followed by a similar greeting by the Principal. It was quite amusing for me to receive such attention/recognition in the presence of the entire top management. In the process, everybody from the top management got to know me, even though I didn’t know most of them.

My Branch Manager had noticed that the GMP knew me and strategically planned to make use of my acquaintance with him to his advantage. He told me that the branch wanted to hold a dinner party for the glitterati of the town and asked me to seek the GMP’s approval for it, since it entailed a good expense and the same was not within his powers to sanction. When we were about to approach the GMP’s suite, he revealed to me the last bit of information that since Kasauli was a cantonment station, most customers of the branch were Army/Air Force officers who did not enjoy dinners unless drinks were served. He also mentioned that the bank’s rules did not permit us to serve liquor, but it could be possible with the GMP’s approval.

The idea worked well and the GMP agreed to the suggestion, with a caveat that liquor expenses should not be on the bank's account. We assured him that we would manage the spending efficiently so that nothing reflects in the branch's expenses for the amount spent on liquor.

The evening arrived and we had a wonderful party. Everybody enjoyed the food, the drinks and specially the attention that they received from the GMP. Everybody who attended the dinner left assured that they could reach out to the GMP whenever they found a deficiency in the bank's services or if the branch was unable to cater to their requirements.

The next morning, as soon as I arrived at the branch, the Branch Manager asked me to accompany him to meet the GMP for conveying our thanks to him. On meeting him, I enquired by way of courtesy if he enjoyed the evening, and asked him how he found the food and drinks there. He responded by saying that he hadn't taken any drinks or food at the party the previous night since there was a lunar eclipse and he, being a Tamil Brahmin, was fasting. Surprised at his words, I retorted, "But I saw you taking drinks as well as food."

He laughed and confessed that he didn't say no to the drinks or the food, but clandestinely kept his drink and food plate in some corner so that nobody could notice it.

It was an astonishing eye-opener for me. It was quite usual in our family or circle of friends to fuss over food or demand specific drinks of choice. Astoundingly enough, the GMP had not consumed even a morsel of food or a sip of drink, and nobody had any clue about it. It was a great learning for me. This incident got so ingrained in my mind that I made it a point thereafter to ride the tide and enjoy people's company, irrespective of the quality/quantity of food or drinks served.

This lesson in etiquettes has stood me at a vantage point throughout my professional life.

I often narrate this anecdote to my juniors when they say no to an offer of tea without giving a thought to the fact that perhaps the person who is making the offer wants to enjoy the same in his/her company or just wants to make the other one comfortable and is ready to spend his/her valuable time in hosting a cup of tea.

10

NO PROBLEM

After my first branch training at Kasauli since joining State Bank, I got the second branch posting at Chambaghat, a small town near Solan–a district headquarter in Himachal Pradesh.

Since it was a small branch in a very small town, most of the staff stayed at Solan, which was about three kilometers from Chambaghat, and we walked to office everyday in the pleasant weather of the hilly town. The summers there were nice and cool too. Houses in those days did not even have fans, let alone air conditioners.

More often than not, we would finish our work within the office hours and have long evenings to spare after 5 o'clock. Unless one had a creative hobby or some other activity planned, evenings could become very boring for a single person staying away from his/her family. During that time, I came in contact with a few important personalities of the town who offered that I join the Rotary Club there. When they got to know that I was just about 24 years old, they suggested that I join the youth wing instead, i.e., Rotract Club. I joined the club and was asked immediately to take over as the Secretary, since the club had become almost defunct with no members active. I agreed to it and started initiating activities which were usually pursued by the Rotary Clubs.

However, that didn't satisfy me. I wanted to do a big event to have the club gain some popularity and attract membership. We parleyed with the Rotary Club President and took his guidance on the activities and events that could bring life into the club. Finally, we resolved to hold State Level Tournaments in Table Tennis. My colleagues, who held executive positions in the Rotract Club, were quite apprehensive about hosting such a big event and tried to convince me to go for smaller activities, viz., tree plantation or a blood donation camp which didn't require a lot of involvement or financial expenditure. But I didn't want to hold an event just for the sake of it. My target was to make the people of the State realise our existence and know that the Rotract Club of Solan had the ability to hold a State Level Tournament. When you grow up, you acquire a better perspective to look at the risks involved, but youth gives you the advantage to go where your heart guides you, unmindful of the challenges involved.

When we set out to carve out a plan and arrange for the wherewithals, my colleagues started expressing the difficulties involved. At every step, their effort was to dissuade me from holding the tournament. But every time they came up with a problem, I would utter, "No problem," and provide a solution to it. They would often laugh at my approach, but when implemented, they discovered that it was perhaps the best alternative under the given circumstances. Moreover, we had a lot of support from the Rotary Club of Solan, by way of guidance as well as financially.

Once we had decided and I got the go-ahead from the Rotary members, I issued a press release in my capacity as the Secretary of Rotract Club, which

ROTRACT CLUB
STATE TABLE TENNIS TOURNAMENT
SOLAN

was published prominently on the sports page of the newspapers. Only print media existed at that time, while TV and Radio didn't carry any commercials. Solan, for that matter, didn't have TV in those days. A tremendous response came from the universities/ colleges of different districts, putting an end to our worries regarding receiving adequate participation. The real challenge became the arrangement of boarding and dining facilities, which was the next step and entailed a big expense if it were to be arranged at a hotel.

God's blessings came timely, as always, and I got to know that the SP of police in Solan was an ex-State Bank person. He had joined State Bank as a probationer a few years back, but when he got selected in the civil services, he opted for the latter and left State Bank to join the Indian Police Services.

I asked my colleagues to set up a meeting with him. When we told him about our plans and my background, he readily agreed to support us and ordered his assistant to have the Govt. guest houses in Solan available for the participants to stay and eat at, that too at very nominal charges as were paid by the government officials. At my request, he also agreed to give a valedictory address and grace the prize distribution ceremony at the conclusion of the tournament.

Despite such support, there were incidents and situations which we had not anticipated. Some participants came with their own demands, some didn't find the accommodation arrangements satisfactorily comfortable, there were frequent arguments/quarrels amongst the participants too. At times, we would go rushing to the Rotary Club senior functionaries and resolve the issue as per their guidance. But my 'No problem' comment had become very popular by then and whenever there was a dispute, they asked the person to approach the 'No problem' guy.

Press representatives would often approach me for a press release, especially after the games reached the quarter final stage. Thereafter, a daily press release became a routine and we came to the finals soon.

A big crowd came to watch the finals and the tournament concluded with the selection of the best players in Men's, Women's, Doubles', and Mixed Doubles' category. The Rotary Club's governing members were on cloud nine that such a big event, that the entire town was talking about, had been organized under their patronage. The administration also applauded the efforts made for bringing in a competitive culture of sports to their hill-state. The SP of police delivered a valedictory address, applauding Rotract Club Solan for having hosted a State-Level Tournament so successfully.

Before we came to the Finals stage of the tournament, I had completed my tenure at the branch. In fact, I received my transfer orders merely two days prior to the Finals. When I shared this news during my address to the gathering that I was to leave the town soon, there was a murmur of protest and some officials even offered to approach the management to hold the transfer. But I requested that no management liked interference, and I was only a trainee at that time, so I needed to finish my training schedule.

After I left Solan, my colleagues at the club planned some activities on their own but the difficulties often surmounted their efforts and they even had to abandon the event at times. They made an effigy reading my catchphrase 'No Problem' and set fire to it.

Life has to move on and I moved on to a new location with a new posting as well, but I vividly recall those challenging days and the achievements of my Rotract Club stint. It was all due to the blessings of the Almighty, that I could plan and hold such a big event. Truly, when blessings come, everything appears easy to handle.

11

SISU

'*Sisu*' actually means your strength lies in your gut, literally. When someone has *sisu*, it means he or she encompasses extreme perseverance and dignity in the face of adversity.

This word actually describes my approach towards some of life's situations. I had started working at State Bank which had well laid out systems and procedures to deal with matters. But then, being a human, I couldn't compromise with my own convictions which I had imbibed during the course of growing up in a family where certain values were ingrained so deeply that it was not possible to go against them and change my track. Even though my seniors directed me to handle certain situations in a particular way or to act as per the bank's laid down systems/procedures, I challenged the same and persevered to handle the situations my way. Perhaps it was the way I had been brought up which gave me the courage and conviction to put my foot down.

The story goes back to the time when I got posted in a small town in U.P. as Branch Manager. When I first received the orders for this posting, I wasn't too inclined to move to such a small town, specially after having lived in Delhi for most of time in my life. One of my friends who was studying with me at Law Centre Delhi offered that we visit Firozabad and assess the situation first hand. He offered to drive us in his car. Upon landing in the town, we went to the State Bank branch and interacted with the Branch Manager and staff there. A few customers came to meet me too when they got to know about the change in incumbency and of my presence in town that day. My friend opined that had he been in my place, he would have liked to take the position. I was about thirty years old then. He said that it would be anybody's dream to become a Branch Manager, that too at State Bank, at such a young age and with ample prospect to rise to a very high position in future. At his suggestion, I decided to agree to joining the assignment and submitted my joining report to the Branch Manager, intimating that I would join after about a fortnight and take charge thereafter.

On our way back, however, my wife announced that she would not like to move to such a dingy small town and proclaimed that it would be difficult for her to adjust to the kind of life that this place had to offer. I assured her that I would try for a cancellation of my transfer.

Once back in Delhi, I met with my seniors through Officers Association and was asked to submit a representation giving plausible reasons for not being in a position to join my new assignment. They assured me that they would take up the matter with the Head Office and try to put the matter of transfer on hold. Unfortunately, however, this was not to be and I landed in Firozabad after a few days, early in January, 1984.

Firozabad is a city in the state of Uttar Pradesh, midway on the Delhi–Lucknow railway route, about 45 kilometres away from Agra – the city of Taj Mahal. It is also known as the *City of Glass* or *Suhag*

Nagri because of its famous bangle making industry which engages most of the population.

It was a mandatory requirement for the Branch Manager to visit all the industrial units at least once in a month to ensure end-use of the funds given, which meant, whether the funds borrowed from the bank were being deployed in the business completely. A small industrial unit there, engaged in manufacturing crystal glass, was availing a limit of Rs. 5000/- from our bank. When I visited the unit for physical verification and interacted with the proprietor of the firm, I got to know that his requirement of funds was much higher, but the previous Branch Manager had not been willing to raise the limit for his unit.

I asked him to submit an application for the enhancement of limit. Since it fell within my discretionary powers, I figured that I should be in a position to sanction him a higher limit, to be worked out as per the bank's laid down system for computation of the working capital requirements. He submitted his application for enhancement of the limit to Rs. 25,000/-. Since it met the laid down criteria, I sanctioned him the higher limit of Rs. 25,000/-. Word went around the entire town that the new Branch Manager could sanction limits in a matter of only a couple of days and could even go to the extent of sanctioning substantial enhancements.

After the limit has been sanctioned, the Branch Manager was required to submit a Control Return (CR) to the Regional Manager, also known as the

Controller, as part of the control system. I submitted the CR as per the requirements, but the same came back with great efficiency within a week and I had directions from the Controller to roll back the limit on grounds of it not being sanctioned as per the bank's norms. An enhancement of 500% could not be justified under any circumstances, as the usual quantum of enhancement ranged between 10 to 20%. I submitted my reply, giving a detailed working and the historical background of the firm, delineating that it had been dealing with the bank for a number of years and there had not been any default in adhering to the bank's discipline. Instantly came the reply that they were of the considered view that an enhancement up to Rs. 7000/- could be granted at most, a forty percent jump, directing me to cap the limit at Rs. 7000/- and send back a confirmation within 7 days of having complied with the instructions.

A few days after I had received the directive to cut down the limit, my controller came to the branch for a visit, a quarterly practice quite meticulously followed by good controllers. My controller had the reputation of being a very fast decision maker, of a strong built and a very sound mind. After he had finished the routine check of the books and other compliance requirements and had reviewed the business growth (which he found quite impressive), I arranged for a sumptuous lunch cooked by my wife, since our residence was right above the branch premises.

It was now time for my calling since my Boss appeared to be quite satisfied with my performance in all respects. I mentioned to him about this directive of reducing the limit from Rs. 25,000/- to Rs. 7,000/-, which he feigned ignorance of having signed. He asked me to resubmit the entire matter, which I agreed to do, but added a caveat that in case the limit had to be reduced, they should look for another Branch Manager, as I wouldn't be in a position to carry that out. He suggested that I shouldn't make it a personal issue, but assured me that he would do his best to approve of the enhancement.

I received the CR after a week, duly approved and confirming my action of enhancing the limit. Yes, I had had my way. Despite being in the initial stages of my career, I had created a reputation for myself of having '*sisu*' who could even go to the extent of putting his job at stake to have his way. Soon after, I got a more challenging posting as the Branch Manager of a much bigger branch in Delhi.

I was rewarded for taking a stand, rather for being stubborn (sisu).

12

STRANGERS
WHO BECAME FRIENDS

Life comes back full circle; I experienced this in real life at a later stage in my life.

After I completed my post graduation, there was pressure from my family to look for a job. To satisfy their concerns, I applied for jobs occasionally too and found that most of the openings were available in public sector banks. I got selected for clerical positions in some banks, but I evaded the idea of joining on one pretext or the other.

I had applied for a PO job in one of the largest public sector banks–State Bank Group, during that time. On a Sunday morning, the day the written test for it had been fixed, my father woke me up early in the day, reminding me that I had to appear for the test in a few hours. I told him that I was in no mood to sit for the exam, since I had not prepared for it at all. He chided me, saying that I could not waste his money like that and would have to go and write the paper, come what may.

I did go and after crossing the various stages viz., the written test, a group discussion and various interviews, I got selected for the job.

I was in the waiting for the appointment letter and was spending time visiting friends, watching movies and basking in the glory of having been selected for a premium job, since only about 300 persons had made it through the elimination rounds out of a hundred thousand candidates. One afternoon, when I returned after watching a movie, my mother handed me my appointment letter. My delight was doubled when I glanced at the letter and found that I had got my first posting at the Kasauli branch.

Kasauli is a small picturesque town in Himachal Pradesh, a cantonment with the Army and Air Force bases. The town is near Chandigarh, and I had visited a friend in Chandigarh about a month before; a friend from Delhi who was pursuing his post graduation from Punjab University at that time. When I had been there with him, he planned a picnic to Kasauli along with his classmates, most of whom were beautiful girls from Chandigarh. Having experienced such a wonderful environment and with such company, you always want to relive the moments as soon as the very thought of having been there flashes in your mind.

After completing the formalities, the medical test, etc., I headed to the corporate office to report to the General Manager, whereafter I headed for Kasauli with my dream to live in a lush green valley, surrounded by hills in all directions.

The initial period was quite eventful as I was told that I shall be attached with a clerk at the front desk for a fortnight to learn about ledger posting. Thereafter, I could handle the front desk independently.

Before joining this job, I had worked for a short stint at another bank in clerical cadre, but I did not share this information with the staff at Kasauli. So, when I was asked to remain under training for a fortnight, it appeared to me that it was going to be very boring, since I had already acquired quite a bit of efficiency in ledger posting at my last job. So, I told my colleague that with my background of an Honours in Physics and a Post Graduate degree in Mathematics, the ledger posting should come naturally to me, and conveyed my appreciation to him for guiding me in such a simple way of going about it. Since he was a local person and had a large number of friends and acquaintances, I persuaded him to go out and enjoy while I did the ledger posting.

I assured him that he could have a look after 2/3 hours and check whether the posting had been done correctly. I applied myself fully to the work doing the ledger posting and by 1.30 PM, all the work was over. He came back to the branch and asked me where all the vouchers were. Astonishment was writ large over his face, as probationers usually took a long time to do posting for the first time. After a random check, he felt very confident and was delighted to realize that he could leave every day and enjoy with his friends, while I slogged at the branch.

My interaction with the customers was very interesting, as most of the clients were either Army or Air Force officers or their spouses; we did not have women in the Army at that point of time. Though the day passed by easily at the branch, as soon as evening dawned everyday, a feeling of nostalgia and melancholy would set in.

One of the days, I was feeling a little nostalgic about my family and was lost in my thoughts when a lady customer walked over to my counter, wished me and handed over a withdrawal form to withdraw some money. I promptly handled the transaction and personally took the token, collected her payment and handed it over to her. She gave me a detailed introduction of herself, Ms. Baweja, and enquired about me, my family and my education background.

Once she learnt that I hailed from Delhi, just as herself, she extended an invitation for dinner to me for the next day. I hesitated about accepting the invitation and told her that I had shifted in with another person from the State Civil Services, and it might not be appropriate on my part to visit somebody sans his company. She immediately responded that I could bring that person along and left without giving me a chance to decline the invitation.

That evening, I checked with my partner for dinner the next day and he readily agreed to accompany me. The next morning, Mr. Baweja came to my branch and introduced himself, confirming the invitation.

We had very interesting conversations besides the delicious food, and the most interesting part of the conversation was shared by Ms. Baweja. She told us that after she had qualified her LLB examination from Delhi University, she enrolled for practice with the Bar Council of India, but she did not get any clients for about a month initially. Then one day, a client approached her for getting bail for a relative of his, and briefed her about the incident. She took the engagement as her counsel and drafted the bail application.

When she appeared before the judge, he asked her to put forward the defence for the grant of bail. Since she was appearing in court for the first time, she did not know a lot about the court rules and proceedings. She went very close to the judge and whispered in his ear, "*It is my first case and I do not know what defence should be put forward.*"

She beseeched him to grant the bail, and to everybody's surprise, the judge accepted the application and granted the bail. The client was so happy that he paid her a good amount of money in addition to the agreed fee.

That was a wonderful age to live in as people were very transparent and forthright. Even though it was a first meeting, she didn't hesitate to share this embarrassing yet amusing anecdote with a stranger. When such lovely relationships are made, I am reminded of the quote by W. B. Yeats:

There are no strangers here; only friends you haven't yet met.

13

THE HONEST CAB DRIVER

Mumbai is really a megapolis. There is no other city in the world which can match up to the diversity that Mumbai offers as a city.

Here, you will find people who live in small *chauls*; big families of 8 to 10 members surviving in a small room with the bare minimum supply of electricity and no water. They are required to stand in long queues to fetch even a single pale of water, and even then it is available for barely an hour during the day.

On the other hand, there is South Mumbai which takes pride in its plush bungalows belonging to celebrities and rich businessmen who compete with the best in the world.

Mumbai has its own soul which surprises you when you chance upon to witness it. One such experience of mine with the lesser mortals of the city is unforgettable for me and is reproduced here in this story.

I have been a frequent visitor to Mumbai and stay there for a while each time I visit, ranging from one to ten days at a time. The first time I travelled to Mumbai was in the year 1975, when I had to appear for an interview at the BARC (Bhabha Atomic Research Centre). Being a distinction holder with an Honours degree in Physics, I was eligible to appear for an interview with the BARC for the post of a Scientist Officer. Most of my classmates who had cleared B.Sc. Physics Honours had decided to appear for this interview so that they could make a sojourn in

BHARAT CO
DEEWAAR
XEROX

Mumbai for all costs being borne by BARC. A round trip fare in first class was reimbursed by BARC for all those who had been called for an interview for this post.

Young and fresh out of college, the free trip to Mumbai was a more fascinating prospect than pursuing a career with B.A.R.C. We booked our tickets to Mumbai in a fast mail train right away. During the journey, we met a family which warmed up to us quite nicely and we shared food and good conversation with them throughout the journey. When we got down at Mumbai, we even shared a taxi, since we all were to travel in the same direction. The destination of our co-passengers, however, was before ours.

We bid them goodbye upon reaching their residence and embarked onwards on our journey. We had only gotten a little distance further when I heard somebody yelling 'stop-stop'. I asked the driver to stop and saw that the gentleman who had been our co-passenger was running towards our taxi. I got down and enquired of him whether he had forgotten some item in the cab. He rebutted, "No no, it is nothing like that."

He then told us that he worked with a film production company and had hid this fact from us fearing that we would ask him to arrange for us to see a live shooting. He mentioned that his wife had chided him for it, that instead of making an offer to us to go to his studio and watch some shooting, he had hid this fact from us. She had not liked it at all. He had thus come running after our cab to make amends for his mistake. We thanked him profusely and told him that since we were staying with some relatives who were in the movie business too, we would have ample opportunities to see movie shootings anyway.

This act of our co-passenger impressed me a lot, since an average North Indian would not have given a damn about it, specially when the journey had been completed and everybody had proceeded to their respective locations.

Thereafter, whenever I visited Mumbai, I met people, befriended them and found them very caring, despite the fact that my pocket was once picked in a local train there.

The next anecdote which I am going to share is about a taxi driver. I had a few hours to spare before my flight from Mumbai and I decided to take time to meet a friend who had his office in Fort Mumbai. After exchanging some usual chit chat, he asked me if I would like to visit some place around there. I had been told by another friend of mine that there was a garment shop nearby which had gents' trousers and shirts at very reasonable prices, but with the tag of a big brand. The stuff was apparently very good too. In those days, shirt brands had not become very popular and buying a branded shirt for a very reasonable price appeared to be an attractive proposition. The usual practice was to get a tailor to stitch your shirts customised to your exact size.

The garment shop was about three to four kilometers from his office and we decided to take a taxi to it. We signaled for a taxi and boarded it even before the driver made the enquiry of where we were to go. After we had settled comfortably inside, the driver asked us about our destination and conveyed us to the garment shop in the next ten minutes. The driver asked for a fare of Rs. 18, and we paid him a Rs. 20 note. He fumbled in his pockets for spare change, but could not find any to return to us. We thanked him and went into the garment shop.

After we were finished with the shopping, we came out and saw a taxi waiting outside. We signaled and boarded it right away. The driver started heading towards our destination, without even enquiring about the place that we were to be dropped at. I got a little suspicious and looked at the rear view mirror to see the driver's face. I then looked towards my friend who mentioned that this driver appeared to be the same one who had brought us there. When I looked at the driver through the rear view mirror again, he muttered, "Sir, I am the same driver. I waited for you outside the shop. I figured that after your shopping, you would want to go back to your office. Since I din't have the change to pay the balance money of Rs. 2, I waited outside so that the amount could be settled over the return journey."

We felt really amused and befuddled at the level of his honesty and expressed great appreciation for him. We did reward him, which he accepted with much reluctance.

From that day on, I started having great respect for the denizens of Mumbai, and it dawned on me that the character of a city is judged by the morality of the lowest rung of the society. It is the duty of all of us to ensure that they get their due in their day-to-day interactions with us and the rest.

12

DO UNTO OTHERS

WHAT YOU WOULD HAVE THEM DO UNTO YOU

We landed in Goa and looked forward to a good stay, as it was monsoon time, with the season in its last leg. We looked forward to enjoying the rains in the hotel, as there were only two families there at that time; mine and the family of another friend of mine who had tagged along with us from Bengaluru. Our travel, which started from Delhi, had already taken us to Mumbai –Bengaluru–Ooty–Cochin–Trivandrum – Kanyakumari and then had brought us to Goa. We were both working in State Bank then and our travel plans those days were decided keeping in mind the reimbursement for fares given (as per the eligibility in the entitled class) up to the last point touched. In line with that, most of us residing in North India usually had Kanyakumari as the final destination.

To my utter surprise, when I met my colleague, Mr. Seth, in Bengaluru through another common colleague, I found that he had not planned out his itinerary except for the fact that he had to touch Kanyakumari so as to make himself eligible for the maximum reimbursable amount. When I shared my itinerary with him, he suggested that we travel together since all of us (his family and mine – each having four members; two adults and two kids) could pack in one car, making it more economical for both of us.

In Goa, Seth's friend had a hotel which was undergoing renovation, nonetheless two rooms were made ready for us to stay in.

We found that the hotel rooms were quite large and very tastefully renovated, and the Goa trip started off on a good note. When you know that you do not have to pay for your stay, you do not care to plan for the number of days spent there. Yet, we planned to leave after a week. Mr. Seth had air tickets confirmed for his travel from Goa to Mumbai, while I had my tickets wait-listed. In those days, the only airline that provided air connectivity was Air India. They had this policy of waitlisting some passengers against cancellations, after they had made bookings for the number of seats available in the aircraft.

When I got up the next morning, I read in the newspaper that a shipping company had started their cruise services on the Goa-Mumbai route. I figured that it was a good opportunity to add another feather to our travelogue by having the experience of travelling by sea. Since my tickets were waitlisted anyway, I decided to cancel them immediately. When Mr. Seth got to know about my plan, he also decided to cancel his tickets, even though they were confirmed.

From one family, we were now two families without any confirmed tickets, aspiring to enjoy a sea-journey for the first time, Seth and I went to the office of the shipping company to make bookings for the Goa-Mumbai trip. We approached the booking official and requested him to book our tickets for the journey to be undertaken the coming week. He told us that the cabins were all booked for the next three months, but we could travel on the deck, for which no booking was required, and we could travel

on any day, however with the caveat that kids would not be allowed to travel on the deck. Seth was very perturbed on coming to know about this, and he put the entire blame on me for having cancelled his confirmed tickets.

I appraised the situation and told him not to panic. I checked the credentials of the booking officer; his name was Ramesh and he had the authority to accommodate new passengers against open seats and cancellations. I approached him and shared with him our predicament, that we were bank officials and had cancelled our air tickets as the idea of a sea journey fascinated us. Though we had a place to stay for even a couple of months more, we could not remain away from work for such a long period. Moreover, we had school going children. I beseeched him to come to my rescue as my colleague was very angry with me for coming up with this idea and for making him cancel his air tickets.

Ramesh asked me for the details of our travel date and number of passengers etc., and told me to come back after three days. He promised that he would try to give us a booking.

Goa has some of the best beaches in India and we had a fun time visiting different beaches, going into the sea and playing with waves. The children were really exhilarated and had great fun playing water games. While everyone was having fun, my friend Seth appeared to be in a nasty mood and expressed his apprehension to me whether Ramesh would be in a position to give us a booking and was quite skeptical about it. I had no option but to keep reassuring him, keeping my faith in the Almighty.

We landed at the booking office of the shipping line on the designated day and time. Ramesh was busy preparing for the day's journey of the ship which was to take about 19 hours to reach its destination. After the ship sailed off, he came to the office and we approached him urgently, expressing our anxiety. He enquired about my family details and made a ticket for a cabin. I requested him to make booking for Seth as well. He did it nonchalantly. He told me the fare amount, which was really small, for the journey to be undertaken, I took out my wallet and offered to pay him over and above the amount of the tickets, whatever he deemed appropriate for going out of his way to give us the tickets. He responded that we only had to pay the amount as mentioned on the ticket and that there was no need to pay any additional amount. I thanked him profusely, gave him my business card and asked him to contact me whenever he would come to Delhi.

When we walked out of the booking office, Seth was nonplussed. He looked at me in great astonishment. He was quite amused by how Ramesh had helped us, even though we had met him for the first time and had no reference whatsoever. He asked me how I had managed to pull this off. At this stage, I shared with him how I always made it a point to help all my clients who approached me for support when the front desk was not in a position to help them. Most of the time, I sent my customers fully satisfied and they always conveyed their blessings to me. I shared with him my philosophy of doing to others what I want others to do to me.

Seth was so impressed with my approach that he told me that he would always seek my advice whenever he found himself in a tricky situation from then onwards.

We bid goodbye to Goa, carrying with us the beautiful memories of the days spent together in such a salubrious climate and thanking the Almighty for coming to my rescue.

15

TRAVESTY OF LAW

We all have great regard for the Constitution of India and swear by it before taking any position as a member in the State Assembly, as a Parliamentarian, or other constitutional positions.

When it comes to seeking justice in a court of law, however, most of us feel frustrated on account of delay in the delivery of justice. I was in for great disappointment when I got the opportunity to handle a legal matter at an early stage of my career.

I was posted as Divisional Manager (Advances) at a branch in State Bank at that time. It dawned on me that I could improve my career prospects if I pursued a Degree course in Law. The Law Centre of Delhi University fell mid-way on my route to work and the class timings suited me too, as they were held between 6:15 PM–9:15 PM after my office hours. I decided to join the Law course as it could serve the dual purpose of getting a law degree, plus the subject matter of the course could help me prepare for my banking related exams that were mandatory for a promotion to a higher grade.

At this point of time, after I had started attending the evening classes at the Law Centre, Delhi, simultaneously handling the high responsibility position of a Divisional Manager at a large branch, I received an envelope from the court. I opened it to find a decree in a legal suit that the Bank had filed against a professor who taught at a reputed college in Delhi University. A decree is an order of judgement (or decision) given by the court in a case filed by a party against another person. Upon going through the contents, I learned that this professor had availed some credit facility (a small amount of some four thousand odd rupees) from the branch and had refused to repay. The bank was thus constrained to prosecute the professor for the recovery of the amount. However, neither the professor, nor his lawyer appeared in the court to defend their case, and there were *ex-parte* proceedings. In the decree, the court had passed a judgement that an amount of Rs. 17,000/- was payable by the professor to the Bank. The amount had bloated from Rs. 4,000/- to 17,000/- due to the application of interest over a period of about seven years.

I discussed the process for recovering the amount with the Bank's legal counsel. He advised me to send him a copy of the decree, asking him to deposit the amount as mentioned in the judgement within a period of fifteen days. I followed the procedure as suggested and waited for the outcome of the demand notice. No reply came forth to our communication. It greatly puzzled me that a person of such high repute, a professor as well as author of books–that too in the subject of commerce–could be so callous towards his responsibility of repaying the amount that he had borrowed. As a professor, he was drawing a good amount of salary and also earned a fat royalty from his books.

This was tantamount to dishonesty, and I could not come to terms with it and made me want to pursue the course of law to make the recovery.

I discussed again with my legal counsel the process for initiating the steps to make the recovery. He suggested that we file an application for the execution of the decree in court, which meant approaching the court with a request for attachment of the assets owned by the professor. The court would then grant permission and appoint a bailiff – a person of court who would accompany us to prepare a list of the professor's assets, arrange for an auction of these assets, and then realise the proceeds from the sale of the assets. Those proceeds would then be deposited with the bank and appropriated towards the loan amount.

We followed the process and after taking the necessary approvals from higher authority, filed an application in the court for execution of the decree and the appointment of a bailiff. The court accepted our application, passed the order and appointed a bailiff. I approached the bailiff the same afternoon and cajoled him to accompany me to the professor's residence at the earliest for the purpose of attachment of his assets.

We fixed up a date and time and arrived at the professor's place one afternoon after his teaching hours were over. The professor resided in one of the college quarters, the drawing room of which was furnished well with a good sofa-set, a dining table and a carpet. He asked us to take a seat, while sitting down on the floor himself. We stood up as soon as he sat on the floor, since both of us were far younger in age than the professor who seemed to be in his late fifties. He told us not to feel bad about him sitting on the floor in front of us, as there was a technical reason for the same. On our enquiry, he mentioned that most of the furniture items lying in his house were already attached under another court judgement, therefore he did not want to use them. When the bailiff enquired of him the details of this other court case, he told us that the same were available with his counsel, and offered to give us his phone number.

Since the due process of law of making the recovery by the sale of assets had failed, I asked my legal counsel, "What next? How do we recover the amount now?"

He said, "Now, we have to file a criminal complaint in the court, which may order incarceration for a specific period if we can prove in the court of law that the professor has defaulted in the payment, despite having adequate means to repay the amount."

My conscience didn't permit me to go to the extent of getting a reputed professor incarcerated for the default of a small amount of money. I decided not to pursue it any further and sought permission to write off the entire amount.

So, '*let the law take its own course*' is the refuge of the law makers as they are well aware of the limitations of law.

16

THANK YOU

THANK YOU is a word mostly used to convey a feeling of gratitude. Though the word is from the English language, it is understood all over the world by people of most countries.

A 'thank you' that I received during the span of my career holds so much value and has been cherished by me for decades now, that I take great pleasure in narrating the anecdote behind this special word.

I was a desk officer at State Bank in Credit Appraisal Department, or CAD, and interacted with customers whose credit requirement was substantially large–above 50 million in those days. When I first came to the department, I was under the impression that the sanction of credit facilities for such large amounts would be a long drawn out process, running over 6 to 8 weeks. To my utter surprise, however, I found that the credit facilities were sanctioned to the customer the same day at times. The only reservation being that the customer must approach the bank in the reverse order i.e., from top down.

Usually when you need funds from a bank, you approached the branch wherein a clerk/officer briefs you about the process and gives a long list of documents that you have to produce before he processes the loan proposal. Thereafter, it passes through many layers of scrutiny before it sees the light of day–the final sanction.

But in CAD, the clients are big industrialists or MNCs that have direct access to the top management and approach the Chairman/Managing Director

CREDIT APPRAISAL DEPT

straight away. After listening to the details, the latter directs the next functionary to consider the proposal, giving his verbal nod in principle. Thereafter, the file flies from the desk officer to the sanctioning authority with such speed that by the evening of the same day, the desk officer receives the sanction. The company's representative would then appear with a smile, conveying his hold on the authorities, and request you to give the sanction letter. The desk officer would never have the audacity then to postpone the delivery of the sanction to the next day, even if the office hours for that day were over.

I have one such wonderful experience to narrate of handling an MNC client, which always inspired me thereon to handle my work with more efficiency as well as proficiency.

A US based MNC, one of the largest producers of aerated soft drinks, had its dealings with my bank and I was handling their account. The sanctioned limit was about 80 million then. The CFO and other representatives often hinted that their credit requirement had gone up as they were scaling up their operations. Since it was the initial phase of the promotion of their products in our country, they had suffered huge losses. Generally in public sector banks, it was the order of the day that no enhancement in credit facilities was to be considered for a loss making enterprise.

I was assigned the task of making an appraisal of their working capital requirements. The boss called me up and shared the agenda with me. Since the MNC had its corporate office in Delhi, I was told to visit their office to critically examine their financial statements and working capital requirement to determine if the enhancement could be considered.

I studied the details carefully and found that the MNC was incurring a loss of about 200 million every year since they established themselves in India, but the losses were being funded by the principal company based in the USA. I called for the Annual Report of the principal company and was surprised to note that it had huge cash reserves and even had the capacity to fund such losses for a few more years. After I was convinced about the safety of the funds, I set about appraising the working capital requirements and took about two days to come up with a proposal to enhance the working capital limit from 80 million to 200 million. The CFO and the other members of the finance and commercial department were very pleased by it and thanked me profusely. The CFO appreciated my effort and told me that during two years at IIM he did not learn as much as had learned in the previous two days during the process of finalising the working capital limits.

After I returned to HO and shared the details that I had proposed for an enhancement of 150% over the present limit, my fellow desk officers scared me by saying that when the government policies would undergo a change, these MNCs would be compelled to shut their businesses here in India and abandon the country. At that stage you may be in big trouble, they said and warned me as well as convinced me to stay put as far as their credit limits were concerned. However, I went ahead with my conviction and put up the proposal to the management for approval for an enhanced limit. Thereafter, it was got approved by the Executive Committee which happened without a single observation. The sanction was then conveyed to the MNC.

I became a hero overnight as a lot of foreign banks were very keen on taking a share in funding the MNC, and they started approaching me to give them a good share out of the total kitty–the sanctioned limit; the demand surpassed the total available limit.

Since it was a consortium lending (a group of banks coming together to lend, with one bank acting as the leader), a consortium meeting was convened to allocate shares to the existing bankers, as well as the new member banks who had given their consent to lend. The representatives of the new member banks scrambled for a share in the credit limit even before the start of the meeting. When the meeting was about to commence, the CFO approached to tell me that somebody wanted to meet me, and requested me to come out of the meeting room for a minute. When I headed out, I was surprised to find the Chairman of the company waiting there for me. He introduced himself and said, "A BIG THANK YOU, MR. ARORA. I have specially flown down from Mumbai just to say thank you. Though we had been having talks with many other bankers, no body had the courage to appraise our requirements upon knowing that we are a loss-making company." He thanked me profusely and left with a message that I must meet him whenever I visited Mumbai.

I felt on top of the world, for the chairman of one of the largest MNCs in the world had specially flown down from Mumbai to Delhi to convey his gratitude to me for my work.

This THANK YOU is a precious gift which I have cherished for a long time and shall continue to do so.

17

FAUX PAS

Every language has some unique words that are untranslatable in their truest sense to other languages. That is why the English language has absorbed many such words to expand its lexicon.

Faux pas (pronounced as '*fo pa*') is a French word which roughly translates to an embarrassing or tactless blunder. It is often very interesting to recall the faux pas that occur in our life. I am going to narrate one such anecdote from my personal life, which is perhaps one of the best ways to drive home the meaning of this word.

We were visiting Amritsar, the northern-most city of Punjab, which touches the Pakistan border. Before the partition of India in 1947, Amritsar and Lahore were known as the twin cities and were the major trade centres in Northern India. Amritsar had *mandies* for each commodity and every household item, and the areas where these *mandies* were located were named accordingly as *aata mandi*, *namak mandi,* so on and so forth. The *mandies* in this city were the centres of trade of chiefly the agricultural commodities. Amritsar was also a major textile centre since the city had a large number of textile mills and bazars (markets) for selling these items.

Lahore, on the other hand, had upscale market places and was more of a fashion centre. Situated there were a large number of importers who shipped in items from Europe, UK and USA, and sold them to the traders and visitors who came to the city from all parts of Punjab.

When we reached Amritsar, my elder sister reminded me that the son of one of my cousin brothers was to get married sometime during the period of our stay in Amritsar, and she cajoled me to attend the wedding. She vaguely told me the address, but also asked me to check for the marriage party from Attari, a small town near Amritsar and adjacent to the border between India and Pakistan. On the day of the wedding, we were at my younger sister's place as her residence was near the wedding venue. We all got ready to attend the wedding which was to take place in the first half of the day. As per the *Sikh* tradition, the nuptial ties take place in the presence of the Holy Guru (Guru Granth Sahib) and before afternoon. Since we had to attend a marriage party, we decked up accordingly: men in suits and ties, and the women folk in brightly coloured suits and adorned in fancy jewellery.

We reached the venue, as guided by my sister, and checked with the people at the entrance to confirm that the hosts of the party were from Attari. Once sure of it, we walked in confidently to join the wedding celebrations and meet the groom and the bride. However, my brother-in-law who is a foodie, suggested that we first take some breakfast and then proceed to meet our relatives.

The dining area was separately maintained and the names of the items being served were painted on the wall behind the buffet table. Thus, we could check even from a distance what all items were being served for breakfast. We grabbed a plate each and were about to proceed to pick the food items of our choice when my wife called me aside and told me that there was something amiss. She told me that judging by the attires donned by the other attendees of the function, it did not appear to be a wedding celebration. She further implored me to check with somebody whether we were at the correct venue. Soon, similar doubts were shared by my sister, while my brother-in-law had already started to fill his plate with his favourite food items.

I scanned the room for a familiar face, but none of our relatives was to be seen anywhere around. I gathered the courage to approach a gentleman and enquired of him whether the families there had come from Attari to attend the wedding. He immediately retorted, "Wedding!? This is a bhog ceremony." (A bhog ceremony is one that is performed after the demise of a person.)

I realized that a faux pas had occurred and signaled my companions to escape from the place. We rushed out of the dining hall, quite embarrassed.

Once out, we rechecked with some relatives on the phone and were given the name of the resort where the wedding was taking place. Without losing another minute, we got into the car and headed to this resort, which was in fact in close proximity to our location.

What a faux pas it really was! Even today, whenever I recall this incident, I feel embarrassed.

Yet, with faith in the Almighty, we were lucky to escape from the situation unscathed. Faux pas transpire nonetheless and there is no way to avoid such an occurrence.

18

NO GLITTER, BUT SWEETER

Destiny takes you where you have to be. You often don't realise it since the events happen so fast. What may not be imaginable today, becomes a reality the very next day.

Way back in 1984, I was posted in Firozabad as Branch Manager in State Bank. The morning of 31st October started as routine but by dusk, the atmosphere in the entire country had changed entirely. Mrs. Indira Gandhi, the then Prime Minister of India was assassinated, resulting in communal violence against a particular community across the country.

My family and I had gone to a friend's place for dinner that night and while returning to our place, I noticed an unusual eerie silence in the streets. Only a rare soul could be seen out in the open. Though I had heard the news of Mrs. Gandhi having been shot during the day, I had no clue of the events that followed, or that she had indeed died of the wound.

On reaching home, I switched on the radio (TV telecast had not started in Firozabad by then) and found out that Mrs. Gandhi had passed away and there were riots in Delhi and many other cities in the country. Come morning, a mob gathered around our building which housed our branch, as well as my residence on the floor above it. Soon, the mob started pelting stones at the building, hurling them at the window panes of the branch, and at our residence as well. I asked my wife to take my two and a half years' old son and remain in the bathroom while I guarded our apartment, lest some unruly miscreants try to break into it. This lasted for about an hour, but the mob couldn't break into our house. They were ultimately forced to disperse by the police and the riots were quelled for the time being.

After that harrowing experience, I decided that I couldn't continue working in that town. I submitted a representation to my Controller, making a request to transfer me from Firozabad. I requested for a posting in Delhi, as all my relatives lived there, despite the fact that the scale of damage to property as well as the lives lost in riots was substantially higher in Delhi.

I was assured of full support by my Controller, and an officer was deputed to manage the branch, while I continued to guide him from home. I was confident that in light of the unprecedented developments, the management would proactively accede to my request for transfer, but no such orders were forthcoming. One evening, when I called up my Controller to discuss the matter, he expressed that he was not inclined to accede to my request for transfer. I put down the receiver disappointedly.

A few days later, an officer of the bank walked into the branch, carrying a big bag. I was quite astonished to see him. When I enquired of him the reason for his arrival, he looked at me in an amused manner and said, "How is it that you don't know about your own transfer while the entire bank is abuzz with the news that the President of India spoke with the Managing Director for fast tracking your transfer to Delhi?" I didn't react to this and kept quiet about the matter.

Within a couple of days, we landed back in Delhi and I joined my new posting as Branch Manager at the Azadpur Mandi branch. It was one of the dirtiest branches in the city. Located amidst the transport centre of the capital city with trucks plying throughout the day, the dust arising on account of the movement of vehicles made it all the worse. The adjoining building housed a wine shop, which put off the decent people from visiting our branch. Despite all that, when I look back, I feel that the time spent in this branch was the golden period of my career in State Bank.

There were quite a few instances which happened and brought good tidings in my life.

One morning, when I arrived at the branch, I noticed that the premises had not been cleaned and all the staff had assembled at one place. "Why have you all assembled here?" I enquired of them. They replied that the sweeper had not come that day, so the premises had not been cleaned. "I shall clean the premises," I told them and asked them to get me a broom. As soon as I uttered these words, they responded immediately, "We will do the cleaning, sir." In the next ten minutes, the cleaning was complete and all the staff members felt good that they did not need to depend on the sweeper to have a clean premises to work in anymore. I credited them for having shown such a high degree of responsibility and it sent very positive vibrations throughout the team, even though I had only offered to clean and didn't have to do anything myself.

I did take pains during the initial stages of my posting to train my staff, specially on how to deliver good service, so that each customer who visited the branch left satisfied. A few months into my job, things got easier. The staff showed a high degree of enthusiasm to learn and there was tremendous improvement in the application level as well.

One of the clerical staff who had excellent handwriting and handled all the returns and advances, was quite meticulous about everything he did. One day, while signing a statement about the categorization of staff that recorded the number of people from minority communities, scheduled caste, scheduled tribe, etc., posted at the branch, I found the mention of one member under minority community. I stopped, being quite assured that we didn't have any staff from a minority community. I called him and told him, "You have not been very careful in preparing the statement today. We do not have any member from a minority community, while you have mentioned one." He looked at me with a naughty smile in response. When I asked him who it was and why had I not been told about it, he pointed towards me and said, "It's you, sir." It was really an eye opener for me, since I had never felt in my life so far that I represented a different community. Feeling quite embarrassed, I signed the report and my confidence in him multiplied manifold.

I challenged the staff everyday to do a little more work than they did the previous day, and the results were surprising. They discovered the potential to increase their efficiency to a higher level. This enhanced our quality of service to such a degree that the branch acquired a great reputation and started getting four to five new customers everyday who came to open their accounts with us. A stage came when we had to ration out the opening of new accounts and a wait-list system had to be introduced to ensure that we opened only that many accounts that we were in the position to provide service for.

With excellent customer service and meticulous compliance, as the reporting was timely and punctilious, we acquired the status of a top branch in the region. I was elevated to a higher position. After my promotion, I was transferred to a larger branch in the commercial hub of Karol Bagh in Central Delhi.

No doubt, there was resistance from some of the staff members to handle the additional load of work, but they did not dare to express it overtly. But, everybody felt that the change that was coming in their efficiency level was becoming a great asset, this they expressed much later when they met me after years.

I still recall what a wonderful team we had created and how we progressed and excelled together. To this day, some of my colleagues from that branch who are in touch with me after retirement, recall those golden days of our career spent in that congested and dirty premises. From my experience of managing this branch, I learned that the amenities and the surroundings do not matter, what is indeed important is the spirit and enthusiasm that is generated when people work together and become a robust team.

19

MY FIRST BOOK

'When you want something, all the universe conspires in helping you to achieve it.'

- Paulo Coelho

While posted at the Foreign Department, I was nominated to attend a training programme related to Foreign Exchange (Forex) Business. I looked forward to visiting the Staff College at State Bank, Hyderabad, to attend the programme. There was always a charm in being away from the office routine for a few days and spending a relaxed time at the College, then come back fully rejuvenated with a renewed vigour and of course having acquired a better skill set.

With these hopes, I landed in the Staff College and went to the classroom on the very first day of the week long training. Our co-ordinator, a senior banker from SBI, came to the classroom and after an initial round of introductions, distributed sheets of paper which were titled 'Entry Test'. He asked us to write out our answers to the best of our ability and mentioned that this test was just to gauge the areas wherein the faculty should focus, so as to prepare us trainees in acquiring the adequate skill set to handle the foreign exchange business after we returned to our desks.

We all wrote the test and returned our sheets to the co-ordinator, after which we had a tea break. The co-ordinator promised that while we enjoyed our tea, he would mark the sheets. After the tea break, he came back to the class fully charged, now with full knowledge of our understanding of foreign exchange as well, and started distributing the answer sheets back to us so that each one could know where one stood. He did not return my sheet and said, "I have a problem with you, Mr. Arora. You should not be attending this programme."

I entreated him with a request not to send me back as I had been looking forward to spending a good time at the college and had been nominated for this programme after a long time. He mentioned then, "Your score in the Entry Test is the highest in class. No participant has ever scored such high marks even in the Exit Test which is conducted at the end of the course to gauge the learnings from the training programme." He expressed his apprehensions regarding whether I would learn anything new during the training. Moreover, I could be a spoilsport in class with my level of knowledge. He asked me to promise that I wouldn't disturb the sessions during the programme and would support him, if need be, to take some topics that the faculty didn't have enough exposure in. I gave him an unconditional undertaking for the same and a tacit understanding for mutual support was made.

The same evening, the co-ordinator invited me over for a cup of tea at his residence, as he had a staff quarter within the College campus. Over a cup of tea, he told me that I had good knowledge of banking–especially foreign exchange, which was a rarity–since very few people got the opportunity to work in that vertical. He told me that I should share my knowledge with others and suggested that I write a book in simple language so that everybody found it easy to handle forex transactions, which were considered quite esoteric otherwise. The idea of writing a book had never occurred to me before, but this got me thinking. I decided to prepare an index, listing the areas of Forex that would need to be covered in case I did embark upon writing a book. I started spending my evenings at the library, figuring out the contents of the book.

Once back from the training, I got busy with my routine and the plan of writing the book hatched at the Staff College was almost forgotten. A few days thence, a friend of mine called me up and asked me to attend with him a book release event that was being presided over by Mr. Atal Bihari Vajpayee, who in later years became the Prime Minister of India. The book was on environmental pollution, authored by the then Chairperson of the Centre for Science and Research. Since the issue was of high importance, I agreed to attend the function. While returning from the event, I mentioned to my friend that I had plans of writing a book myself. Immediately, he mentioned that his brother-in-law was a publisher and offered to speak to him on my behalf. He reminded me that I had met him previously at the wedding function of his cousin sister who had gotten married to this very publisher.

He set up a meeting with this publisher, who asked me to come with the index (of the book) and a preface. When I met the publisher, he agreed to publish the book and the ball was set rolling.

In a couple of months, the book got published and the entire lot was sold out over the next few months. My publisher was surprised. He had never imagined that a book in this field by a novice like me, whose name nobody had heard, would be all sold out in such a short spell of time.

I realized then that the execution of ideas becomes automatic when blessings come. Everything falls into place when you go on with the faith that you have the blessings of the Almighty with you. These blessings have come whenever I have ventured to embark upon a new project, otherwise my academic background of Physics and Maths had no connection with the field of banking, or the specialized field of foreign exchange.

20

ANGUISH OF A LITTLE GIRL

Prague is capital to the largest city of Czech Republic, lying on the banks of the beautiful meandering river Valtva that reflects the golden spires of the 9th century castle that dominates the city's skyline. The historically rich ambience is combined with a certain quirkiness that embraces the entire city.

The city's archaic architecture, rich culture and the narrow winding streets are a testament to its centuries old role as the capital of the historic region of Bohemia. Prague presents itself as a changeable city which likes to alternate styles: it is romantic and successful, both ancient and modern at the same time. Above all, it is a city that is cosmopolitan through and through and is used to welcoming foreigners. The fact that Prague is one of the most beautiful cities in the world can be gauged from the statistics of the tourists visiting Prague. In the year 2016, 7.07 million people (while the population of Prague is 13 million) visited Prague. In comparison, the number of tourists visiting India in 2016 was 8.89 million (the population of India being 1,250 million).

My first visit to Prague was in the late nineties, when I first planned to set up business in Czech Republic. At that time, we were given to understand that it was an unexplored city from a business perspective and had a fertile market for goods exported from India. Indian handicrafts, brass items and hosiery were in great demand. I could speak English well and was under the impression that Prague being a capital city in Europe, most people there must understand and speak English quite well. In my interaction with the people, however, I found that most of them knew little English, limited to general greetings and go-to phrases. They speak Czesky which was the only language that most people there knew.

Besides being one of the most beautiful cities, Prague has the most beautiful girls too; that I found out when I decided to appoint a secretary for myself. With no knowledge of the local language, I found it necessary to hire a local person who could help me communicate and guide me with the local customs, practices, rules and regulations. Though I required to appoint only one girl as my secretary, a bevy of beauties showed up for the interview. What astonished me was that some of these girls were so beautiful that they could give even the girls in beauty contests a run for their money.

Naturally, I selected the most beautiful girl who also happened to be the most suitable for the job, since she had the experience of having worked with expats before and had good command over the English language. This was my primary requirement, the beauty was a bonus.

A few days after landing, I was required to travel to another city, Brno, which held most of the international exhibitions. The city is about 180 kilometres from Prague. I couldn't help but wonder what a tough time lay ahead of me, commuting to Brno everyday, but my staff came to my rescue. They drove me while I was in Czech Republic and told me, much to my surprise, that if we left at about 7.30 in the morning, we shall reach Brno before 9.30 AM. I was surprised at the road infrastructure that enabled us to cover that distance in less than two hours.

At the exhibition in Brno, I became the centre of attraction as most of Czech Republic's denizens had not come across a Sikh before. It was very difficult to make them understand that I wore a turban not to decorate myself, but out of religious compliance. The people there were quite impressed that I made such great effort to look good. I was the cynosure of most visitors there who requested to be photographed with me. While in India, it was a cause of eyebrows being raised when one spoke to or shared greetings with a stranger, but here, every girl wanted to embrace me, hug me and get clicked with me. I found the people here so full of warmth and innocence that when I compared them with Indians back home, I realized how very cunning and selfish we were.

On a Sunday during season time, we planned to head to the office since we had received a consignment from India and the items display was to be made well in advance so as to be ready to receive customers the next morning on Monday. Usually, all of us left our place together and carpooled to the office, but since I was feeling a little lethargic, I told my colleagues to head on without me, assuring them that I would take the metro and join them in a while. They explained the route from the metro station to our store to me so that I would reach there without getting lost on the way.

I took a metro to go to office, but I missed the station where I was supposed to disembark. Realizing it soon enough, I got down at the next metro station and decided to walk back to the previous station, since I knew my way to the store from there. Unfortunately however, I lost the track and figured that I was not going in the right direction to reach my office.

I looked around to find some locals who could tell me the correct route. Luckily, I spotted two girls, one about 12 years old and the other perhaps around 15, and approached them to make my enquiries. Since I knew very little czesky, I could only communicate in English, but they didn't seem to understand any English. I took out my business card and showed it to them, but they still found it difficult to direct me in the correct way.

I wondered and reproached myself for not having made the effort to learn the language of the land where I was starting my business. I said goodbye to the two girls, signalling to them that communication was not possible between us as we couldn't understand each other's language. At that moment, I noticed a peculiar remorse and anguish in the eyes of the younger girl, as if she was blaming herself for not knowing the English language. She seemed to be feeling bad that had she known English, she would have been in a position to help me find my route. It made me realize a human being's natural inclination to help another person.

Eventually, I wracked my brain and found the correct way to reach the office, but the anguish in the eyes of that girl haunts me to this day. It has remained in my mind all this time, reminding me of the care and concern that can come even from a complete stranger in a different country on another continent.

21

THE CAR THAT CHANGED MY LIFE

It is a popular belief that a new entrant to your family can bring a great change to your fortune. In our case, it was a car that put our life in a swift mode, and the car was a Maruti Suzuki SWIFT.

However, it wasn't before undergoing long deliberations on which car to choose. There is always a difference of opinion on which car is superior and the choice generally weighs towards one with a better visual appeal than the functionalities, which should actually find the maximum weightage in the process of selection. After having zeroed in on a Maruti Suzuki Swift, my son and I went to the showroom early one morning to pick the new car. I usually found it tough to drive a new vehicle, so after taking the delivery, I told my son to use the new car, while I chose to go to office in the older one. When it came upon to decide the number, we chose 7650, divisible by 9, which was considered to bring good luck.

I had to attend a review meeting at the Zonal Office the same day. I was the Branch Manager at the Noida branch of State Bank at that time. Such meetings were considered very boring as the Management was never satisfied with your performance and always asked for more. Though my branch had done reasonably well in most areas, we had not achieved the expected targets in the 'Institutional Liability' segment. When I was asked to explain the reason for this shortfall in business accretion, I mentioned to the Zonal Manager that the situation was so because the rates quoted by us, as decided by the Corporate Office, were not competitive enough. The business development in this segment was solely driven by rates and unless we quoted rates better than the other bidders, we would not be in a position to get more business.

In Public Sector banks, however, you were asked to do the impossible, while the top management avoided sticking its neck out for most business related decisions. To survive and go up the ladder, one had to be a yes man–which I was never prepared for. Soon after the performance of my branch had been reviewed, I excused myself from the meeting by requesting the Zonal Manager that there were some urgent matters at my branch that required my immediate attention. He granted me the leave of absence after extracting promises from me that I would make more efforts to achieve the business targets over the next quarter.

While driving back to my branch, I did not feel very good about the way the events had unfolded that day, though the morning had started off on a good note with the newly purchased car. We wished for it to bring more mobility to our lives so we could venture out of the city more often to visit the nearby hill stations. I had proposed to my son and wife that we meet at Gurudwara Bangla Sahib in the evening, and after expressing our gratitude to the almighty, we dine out at one of the high-end restaurants at Connaught Place.

My emotions were running high as I had always worked hard to surpass my business targets, yet

I had been reprimanded for no fault of my own. I looked towards the sky and muttered, “I don’t want to work in this organization any more.” Perhaps, my prayer was heard by the almighty. Soon thereafter, life changing events started to unfold at such a fast pace that when I look back on it now, it gives me tremendous ecstasy.

A few minutes after this silent prayer was made, I received a call from a friend at the Head Office who gave me the news that I had been transferred to Mumbai. He enquired whether I had made a request for a transfer, since transfers to such far off places (for those of us based in Northern India) were made either on request or to punish for non performance. I told him that I had not made any such request, but since it was the management’s prerogative, I must accept it.

It scared me to share the news with my wife, but on coming back to my office, I mustered up the courage and called her to give her the news of my transfer. As expected, she was put off and asked me to cancel our evening plans of visiting the Gurudwara and dinner, but I insisted that we keep the plans as they were and not to let the news have an impact on our plans.

What we had not realized was that the process of change had begun and the new Swift had put our life on a swift mode itself. The events that followed thereafter brought a great transformation to our lives.

The next morning when the family gathered for our morning cup of tea, my wife suggested that we return this car, as it had brought such misfortune with it. Just a few hours after its delivery, this transfer bomb shell had rocked our lives. Since I had purchased the car through a close contact, the possibility of returning was not entirely off the table and I assured her that I would speak to the dealer. My son, however, was not in favour of returning the car, since he was fascinated with the idea of being able to drive to his new office in it. He had joined his job only about a week before and it certainly put him at a vantage point to be driving to work in a new car. Another suggestion that came from my wife was that I should leave the job altogether. She said that I would not be comfortable travelling in Mumbai's local trains and that I should not even deliberate on the idea of driving my own car in Mumbai, as even a one way journey would take about two to three hours.

I made up my mind to look for another job. I knew the Chairman of an auto component manufacturer group, as his office was close by and I used to meet him occasionally. I called him up and mentioned that I would like to meet him. He told me that he was in Switzerland at that time and would return in a couple of days, then perhaps he could drop in to meet me.

Two days later, I received a call from the Chairman's secretary, informing me that he was back and enquired whether he should come to see me. I immediately retorted that I would come and meet him instead. She then told me that a car would be there outside my office in ten minutes.

Upon meeting him, I told him about my transfer and conveyed to him my decision of leaving the job. He suggested that I should not leave such a good job as I had bright prospects of going up the ladder, but I told him that the posting didn't suit me personally. Without losing another moment then, he offered me a position in his company, but mentioned that I would have to relocate to Chennai for it.

As I mentioned before, blessings came and I was given a very senior position, Vice President, with the responsibilities of a corporate head of the entire southern zone, without even having to submit a CV for it. When I landed in Chennai, I happened to find residence in a posh area named 'Ranjit Road'.

When I look back, I marvel at the power of prayers. As soon as I had made my prayer, conveying my feelings of discomfort in continuing my old job, life changing events unfolded at such a fast pace.

Not only did I get a top management job with a higher status, but also a chauffeur driven luxury car and a far more enhanced pay-package than I had been getting at my previous job.

This car indeed proved to be my lucky mascot.

22

THE PERKS OF BEING A SENIOR CITIZEN

Dealing with government departments as well as bank officials is a tough task. In order to avoid it, most of us look for a middleman who, for a hefty fee, could get the work done. While we have gotten used to such a system, the fee demanded by middlemen is so high at times that one prefers to make a try on one's own.

I had purchased a car in 2009 and got it financed from my bank–the State Bank. Since I had a good cash flow, I paid back the entire loan amount within a period of one year. The bank HP, however, continued as I could not find the time to get it cancelled. Eight years passed like that and the stage came when I wanted to sell the car. I was aware that unless the bank HP was cancelled, it would be difficult to find a prospective buyer.

It was the month of December, 2016, post the demonetization period, when I embarked upon this enterprise to get the HP cancelled after collecting the necessary details regarding the process involved. I tried to find a proper middleman, but in that post demonetization period, all such middlemen had disappeared from the market just like the notes of old currency. Thus, once I had taken the decision and got the documents ready, I visited the Transport Authority office, which was luckily just a stone's throw from my residence.

There was a serpentine queue at the entrance gate of the Authority Office, that got me having second thoughts regarding whether I would have the patience to stand through such long queues which I would probably find at all the counters. I made up my mind, however, and took my position in the queue. Soon after, a person approached me and said, "Sir, you appear to be a senior citizen. You don't have to stand in this queue."

For the first time in my life, the benefit of being a senior citizen felt palpable and I rushed through the gate to submit my documents inside. Again, there was a long queue at the counter and I stood in line, forgetting my senior citizen's license. To my delight, the gentleman who had reminded me of my advantageous status outside the building came to my rescue again and announced to all who had gathered there to make way for me. I reached the window where everybody was scrambling to draw the attention of the attendant to themselves.

Now with my exalted status, I called out to the attendant and shared with him the purpose of my visit. He took my papers, examined them and returned to me an acknowledgement of the receipt of my documents. He then asked me to come back on Wednesday the next week, by which time the documents would be processed.

I was delighted to have crossed the first hurdle and set the alarm to reappear before the guy the coming Wednesday. Lo and behold, the next Wednesday arrived quickly as if the divine was supporting me in my effort to get the HP cancelled without involving a middleman. All too aware of the benefits of being a

SENIOR CITIZEN
HELPDESK

senior citizen this time, I knew I could directly outdo everyone else as most other people who had come to the Authority were young and ineligible to enjoy the privilege of such an exalted status. I took out the acknowledgement slip that the authority official had given me the previous Wednesday and handed over the same back to him.

He responded equally fast, "The file has not come yet. You may come after a couple of days."

"Today is Wednesday," I responded harshly, "And you told me to come back on Wednesday. Now you are telling me to come back after a few days? This is not acceptable. You must know that I am a senior citizen."

He changed his stance immediately and told me to go to the next window to get my file. I did not agree to do even that and directed him in an even harsher tone this time, "It is your duty and today is Wednesday, so you should have gotten the file beforehand, knowing very well that I would be coming." He was not used to confronting such authoritative retaliation, and told me not to get angry. He conceded to his mistake and agreed to go and get the file himself. He was back in a jiffy, got my signature on a few papers and asked me to deposit the requisite amount to cancel the HP. I was then asked to come after a month to collect the RC along with the cancelled HP.

After a month, I went back again and was prepared to deal with a similar treatment. Only this time, I had acquired the necessary skills to handle the authority staff. After a little running around, I had to put my foot down again and remind the person of my senior citizen status. To this, he immediately took a duplicate print of the document, since the original was lost in transfer from one desktop to another.

It gave me an immense sense of satisfaction that I could break through the red tape of bureaucracy, that too at a place like this, without involving a middleman. Everyone must enjoy the status of being a senior citizen and exercise the authority that comes with it, albeit with a lot of tact.

23

FIGHTING DEPRESSION

Depression, a menace, is the cancer of the soul. Everyday, I read news articles relating to depression with a lot of trepidation. There have been so many instances where world renowned celebrities committed suicide, and the root cause was depression.

Very recently, I read about the death of Anthony Bourdain, a celebrity chef and travel documentarian, all in all a very successful person who committed suicide at the age of 61. As per the news reports, he had been in a dark mood during the days leading up to his suicide. Anthony hanged himself in his bathroom at a hotel in France.

Gladys Bourdain, Anthony's mother, told the New York Times post his death:

> *He had everything, success beyond his wildest dreams, money beyond his wildest dreams. He is absolutely the last person in the world I would have ever dreamed would do anything like this.*

Just a few days before this incident, the popular celebrity designer Kate Spade took her own life in New York, sending shock waves across the world.

Back home in India, the stunning suicide of Himanshu Roy, one of Mumbai's most beloved and idolized police officers, provoked the outpouring of grief and introspection. Two weeks after this incident, another acclaimed police officer, Rajesh Sahni, shot himself with his service revolver in the middle of the day in Lucknow.

In our country, one in five people is afflicted by a mental illness of some form or anther, traditionally or otherwise. While genetic factors form one reason for it, some of its other manifestations include depression, bipolarity, obsessive compulsive disorder, schizophrenia, anxiety disorders, post traumatic stress disorders, etc.

If you observe closely, you will find that within your own circle of family and friends, a few are coping with depression. It is difficult to pin point the triggers – stress, trauma, loneliness, feelings of inadequacy, genetic propensities – and it cuts across nationality, class, gender and age.

Most mental ailments are manageable with a clinical treatment, the family's support and the patient's own will power. Many such afflictions are caused by chemical imbalances that cause the brain to function abnormally. They are inherently physical disorders that are confused for mental illnesses and trigger the associated social stigma. A lack of awareness and education, coupled with the shortage of medically qualified professionals and resources has worsened the situation of such patients, especially in India where there is only one psychiatrist per one million people.

I have had bouts of depression twice in my life and I vividly remember how drastically I lost my confidence and memory during that time. Upholding the responsibility of being the head of the family, while also being posted away from my hometown, I did not come to realise that I had been afflicted with this deadly disease. Had I even gauged the parameters then and shared them with my wife, she would have evaded the issue and suggested that I do not speak to anyone about it.

During those days, India Today had come out with a special issue which focused on the ailments relating to depression. It contained a suggestive list of symptoms along with a methodology to self analyse the extent of one's depression, and the remedies to them. I took the test and found that I had been suffering from mild depression. I used to suffer form a chronic back pain those days. When I checked the medicines that had been prescribed to me for it, I found that I had been given a medicine for depression as well.

I took the decision, there and then, to fight this menace. I threw away all the medicines, for I had understood that my back pain was occurring on account of stress, while this continuous stress had resulted in depression. With the blessings of God, I recovered from this state within a couple of months and the back pain was cured as well.

You have to invoke the blessings of God and they do come. When I got afflicted with this illness for the second time, it became acute. There was massive memory loss, my confidence had taken a toss, and even the smallest of activities viz. driving the car for a short distance appeared to be very difficult and I would try to find ways to evade it. I tried to avoid meeting the people with whom I had interacted so often before. This level of depression manifested itself in other lifestyle illnesses as well viz. high blood pressure, diabetic conditions. I did consult a psychiatrist after a lot of circumspection and reference check on the doctor. It did work well for me and I felt a palpable change in my thoughts soon. Though I didn't go back to the same doctor, I consulted my regular physician who suggested that I should not stop taking the medicine without consultation with a psychiatrist.

A sudden sequence of events soon after changed the situation entirely. We were required to go to Australia, as our daughter-in-law was expecting to deliver her first baby. I was full of self doubt, as was usual during that phase. *Would we get the visa? What information would I give in the columns? Could they find some reason to reject my visa, despite the fact that we had visited Australia four times prior to this proposed visit?*

Blessings came and everything started falling in place. On taking out the visa documents from our last trip to Australia, I found that we didn't need to go for a fresh issuance of visa at all. The previous one still held valid, albeit it was about to expire in a few days. Regardless, we were entitled to enter Australia till the last date of the visa's validity and could stay there for up to three months thereafter. We booked the tickets and flew to Sydney.

God blessed us with a grand-daughter and she proved to be my lucky mascot. I have now completely recovered from my state of depression, and I feel far better charged with an extraordinary level of energy and confidence. It hasn't just been restored, but is at its peak. This I call blessings; they may come to you in the form of a new change, a new entry to your family, be it a vehicle or a new member.

Proper medication under the guidance of a good psychiatrist, meditation and yoga, coupled with a leap of faith is the panacea for depression. There could be tremendous pressure not to talk about one's anxieties, but we risk losing so much more by tying to suppress and hide our vulnerabilities. Summon the courage to be honest about your needs and look at the difficult feelings in the face. With one true companion on your side, be it your parent, your spouse or another kin/friend, you can rise above this menace.

24

THE POWER OF EMPATHY

Empathy is the capacity to understand or feel what the other person is experiencing from within their frame of reference, i.e., the capacity to place oneself in another's position. There are many definitions for empathy that encompass a broad range of emotional states.

Feeling is the most powerful resource we have, while emotions are the life-lines to self-awareness and self preservation that deeply connect us to ourselves and others, to nature and the cosmos. Emotions inform us about the things that are of the utmost importance to us – the people, values, activities and needs that lend us motivation, zeal, self control and persistence. Emotional awareness and understanding enable us to recover our lives and our health, preserve our families, and build loving and lasting relationships.

I was reading Satya Nadella's book 'Hit Refresh' wherein he makes a lot of emphasis on empathy. I quote an interesting portion from his book: During the process of his interview before joining Microsoft, he was asked a question – Imagine you see a baby laying in the street, and the baby is crying. What do you do? Nadella responded, "Call 911." The interviewer walked him out of the office, put his arm around him and told him, "You need some empathy. If a baby laying in the street and crying, pick up the baby."

We have the potential to attain the kind of love we dream of – deep intimacy and mutual kindness, real committed soulful caring – simply because of empathy, our innate ability to share an emotional experience. But to reach the heights of romance, we need all the skills of a high EQ: an astute emotional awareness to make judgements regarding true love and genuine relationships.

Everybody needs empathy. As teachers and parents, it becomes our duty to create situations wherein our succeeding generation acquires empathy, as it would help them have affectionate relationships with everybody around them. When we crib about the behavior of young ones today and find them having a callous attitude towards others, the blame for it has to be taken by us for not creating situations to raise the level of their empathy.

I recall an incident from my banking career that perhaps explains this better. I was passing from the hall outside my General Manager's office and noticed a colleague and good friend of mine, the Chief Manager Personnel Administration, frantically moving to and fro outside the office. He appeared to be very tense and on enquiry, revealed that he always got very tense before entering the GM's office since he was short tempered, loud, intimidating and overbearing, making it difficult for one to speak before him. The same GM was my boss too, but my impression of him was very different. I told him, "Perhaps you have not been able to set up good communication channels with him, otherwise he is one of the most caring persons I have ever come across."

GENERAL MANAGER

I sat down with him there and then and asked him to tell me the nature of his usual interactions with him. He told me the details and mentioned, "When I enter, he signals me to sit down, but I avoid sitting. At times, he asks me if I would like to have a cup of tea, but I always say no to his offer."

I told him, "Today, change your approach and do what I tell you. When you enter his cabin and he signals you to sit down, take a seat right in front of him and greet him with a smile. When he asks for tea/ coffee, say yes and have some small talk with him about the things which you feel are of concern to him in the Bank." I left him with this brief.

A few days later, I encountered him in a similar situation when he was waiting outside the GM's cabin, but without any anxiety or stress this time. He told me, "Your formula worked well and the interaction went exactly as you had mentioned." He was all praise for the GM.

This was the case of two people who wanted to connect with each other, but due to a lack of empathy, the interaction being new, proper communication channels were not set up. As soon as one person was told about the situation, there was an immediate change in his perspective and it became very easy for him to communicate thereafter.

In the initial stages, I also had an altercation with the General Manager when he had joined our department. There was a little error in a note that was put up to the Managing Director (MD). The MD called him and told him about the mistake. He immediately called me and reprimanded me for it. I rebutted, "I admit that I have made a mistake, but the same note has been read and signed by three functionaries in the hierarchy, including you, and it is not appropriate to apportion the entire blame on me." When he still kept on scolding, I told him, "Sir, you can scold me everyday, but then, do not expect quality work from me as your scolding is going to create a very stressful environment in the department." The message went across and he asked me to sit down and offered to discuss the matter over a cup of coffee. We set up a good working relationship thereafter, which has lasted till today, even after two decades. We still speak to each other at least once a month, even though we both have retired and have settled in locations far off.

To conclude, I would like to emphasise that for a good living, not necessarily in terms of monetary achievements, one needs to have three principal attributes: Attitude, Gratitude and Empathy. If we assign a numerical value to each alphabet of the English language, starting with 1 for A, 2 for B and so on, we'd find no other word to sum up to a 100 except the word ATTITUDE. If we add the values assigned as per formula given above, the sum total for this word is :

ATTITUDE = 1+20+20+9+20+21+4+5=100

Having a proper attitude means giving a 100 percent.

Gratitude is another good quality; to express your gratitude for everything that you receive, you must count your blessings and thank the Almighty. Similarly, when somebody is the harbinger of good tidings, we must be grateful and express our gratitude to them.

Lastly, we must have empathy. When we understand the situation from another person's perspective, we are better placed to develop a proper communication channel and do not encounter any difficulty in getting our thoughts and feelings across to the other person. When we have all the three attributes, blessings come in abundance and life becomes beautiful.

25

A GREAT JOURNEY

Here, I would like to share a great experience that I had on a cab journey once.

Life is very uncertain. A time comes in life when neither the person nor his kin want that he/she should live any longer.

A few days ago, Gopal Das Neeraj, the doyen of Hindi poetry, passed away. He portrayed all aspects of life in his poems. He motivated and laid bare the facts of living through his poetry, but in his last moments, he sought permission for euthanasia. A week before his death, he wrote, "My health does not allow me to do anything. My body has become a burden on me and I want to be free from it." He sought the 'helideath' injection to end his life.

An aunt of mine who stayed with her daughter in Jalandhar lived a long life. Suffering from many old age related ailments for many years, she had grown very frail and finally passed away at the age of 92 years. On receiving the sad news of her passing away, I decided that I must pay my homage to her, since she was a very pious lady and had showered great love and affection on us during our childhood. My nephew decided to join me too and booked tickets on the Shatabdi Express, which departed from New Delhi station at 4.30 PM.

The day I had to undertake the journey, I booked a cab to go to New Delhi Railway Station and scheduled my departure from home at 3 PM, as the usual commuting time in the afternoon was about an hour. I booked the cab on a sharing basis to make

NEW DELHI

it economical, since the fare in such a booking is fixed and notified before undertaking the journey, as opposed to booking a cab for a solo journey where the fare is variable, factoring in the distance and time taken to travel.

The cab did arrive, albeit slightly late, at 3.15 PM at my Dwarka residence. When I opened the cab's door to embark, I found a lady already sitting in the cab. It was a Saturday afternoon and I had least expected to find a co-passenger. When I enquired of the driver the reason for arriving late for the pick up, he told me that the lady's booking had come to him prior to mine and he had to go pick her up before coming to my location. When I was told that she had to be dropped at Janakpuri, I got goosebumps. Janakpuri is about eight to nine kilometres away and the route from Dwarka to Janakpuri was generally congested. I figured that it would take a minimum of half an hour in all probability.

I had no choice but to go on, since booking another cab would have entailed waiting for a minimum of fifteen minutes more. I gave the driver a gentle reprimand and told him that I had to catch a train, so he must drop me at New Delhi railway station before 4.30 PM.

We reached Janakpuri at 3.50 PM and had only forty minutes to spare to reach the railway station in time. We had to cover a distance of about 22 kilometres, with all likelihood of congestion in vicinity of the station. I made a silent payer to the Almighty, telling

Him that I desperately desired to be at the prayer meeting to pay homage to my aunt.

The cab driver then told me that he needed to go to a gas station, as the car was running out of gas. I beseeched him to do that after he had dropped me, but he refused, saying that he hardly had sufficient gas to make it to the railway station. He further reasoned that we might get stuck somewhere on the way if I insisted on this. I had no option but to let the driver go to the gas station. I was aware that there would be a long queue, and it was exactly as I had thought. As soon as we arrived at the gas station, I alighted the cab and saw five other vehicles ahead of us at the filling station. I shared with them my urgency to reach the railway station and they were kind enough to permit us to get the filling done for our vehicle before them.

It was already 3.57 PM by then. I had only 33 minutes to make it to the train, but I didn't lose hope, wishing for the departure to get delayed. Now I put full pressure on the driver and told him to drive as fast as he could, jumping traffic signals on empty un-patrolled crossings if need be. He drove fast and by God's blessings, we reached within half a kilometer of the station by 4.25 PM. As expected, the roads were jam packed till the entry point to the railway station and there seemed no chance for me to reach the platform within the next five minutes. I disembarked from the cab and rushed towards the platform. The fare had automatically been debited from my pay account. I reached the platform to find my train still standing there. I heaved a sigh of relief and boarded the compartment nearest to the entry gate. As soon as I stepped on it, the train started moving.

My nephew called me just then to intimate that the train had started moving and that I had missed it. I had constantly been updating him about my location. When I told him that I had made it, he was stunned and thought that I was joking. In the next three minutes, I was seated next to him.

It was God's blessings that made it possible for me to cover that distance in less than thirty minutes, which normally would have taken an hour. The glow on my face thereafter was indicative of the blessings that had been showered on me by the Almighty. When blessings come, life becomes charming and events happen as if somebody is in perfect control of them and is making things happen with such precision.

ABOUT THE AUTHOR

Ranjit Arora is a graduate in Physics (an alumnus of Hindu College) and a post-graduate in Mathematics from Delhi University. He went on to attain a degree in Law from Delhi University as well.

He joined State Bank in 1977 as PO and remained associated with the bank for a little short of three decades. He worked as the Branch Manager at a number of branches, in Administrative as well as Corporate offices. He holds the distinction of having worked in prime positions in Credit Appraisal and Merchant Banking, Treasury as the Chief Dealer (Treasury), in Asset Liability Management as Chief Manager (ALM), and in Forex Operations as Relationship Manager, Manager (SWIFT) and Chief Manager (Foreign Department).

He moved to the corporate world then as the Vice President of Samavardhana Motherson Group, a leading auto-component maker in the world. He took over as COO of Motherson Auto Solutions Ltd., a group company of SMG.

He has previously authored books in the field of banking. His book 'Manual on Foreign Exchange' is reviewed as a treasure trove in the field of Forex by IBA.

Presently, he is engaged in Financial and Legal Consultancy. 'When Blessings Come' is his debut book in the genre of fiction/auto-biography. He lives in Gurgaon, India and has travelled widely across the globe.

You can reach him at:

Facebook: *@whenblessingscome*

Twitter: *@whenblessings*

Instagram: *@whenblessingscome*